Also By Jim Rosemergy

The Seeker

The Watcher

The Third Coming

The Sacred Human

A Recent Revelation

The Transcendent Life

The Quest For Meaning

A Closer Walk With God

Attaining The Unattainable

The Prayer That God Prays

Even Mystics Have Bills To Pay

Living The Mystical Life Today

A Daily Guide To Spiritual Living

How To Be A Wick In God's Candle

THE
GATHERING

A 40-Day Guide to the Power of Group and Personal Prayer

Jim Rosemergy

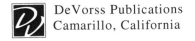

DeVorss Publications
Camarillo, California

The Gathering
Copyright © 2011
by Jim Rosemergy

Bible verses are from the New Revised Standard Version unless otherwise indicated. Interior design by The Covington Group, Kansas City, Missouri. Cover design by Doug Brown, Unity Multimedia Artist.

ISBN: 978-087516-922-4
Library of Congress Card Catalog Number: 2010938685
First Unity Books Edition, 2011
First DeVorss Publications Edition, 2021

DeVorss & Company, Publisher
P.O. Box 1389
Camarillo CA 93011-1389
www.devorss.com

Printed in the United States of America

The Gathering *is dedicated to those who are experiencing the deepest truths of the spiritual life—patience, humility, nonresistance, love and acceptance—by persistently waiting in the Silence. These explorers of the Infinite are my dearest friends. They inspire me to joyously do the work that is mine to do.*

Acknowledgements

My gratitude and deepest thanks to Unity
for its influence in my life and for the staff
of Unity Books, especially Stephanie Stokes
Oliver, whose commitment and support of
this project and editing skills helped to
make available through *The Gathering* a
prayer and meditation practice that
supports the spiritual awakening of the
human family.

Contents

However, this situation is changing. We now know there is a relationship between matter and energy, a relationship between what we see and do not see. There are even researchers who are considering that consciousness and matter share a kinship once thought impossible. I trust that more attention will be given to this area of human endeavor.

As a minister trying to help people with the challenges of life, I have always been interested in the practical application of spiritual principles, ideas and beliefs. Can they, will they help those in need? I have conducted my own experiments to answer these questions. No scientist would endorse my findings, but researchers might be fascinated to know that my laboratory was life. I worked within the confines of my training and experience and with those willing to share life with me, who share the same optimistic viewpoint that there is power yet to be discovered that is available to every human being.

Here is the premise: the power of God is available to each of us. We don't need a scientist to devise an experiment to test this premise; each of us must test the claim for himself or herself. Our lives are the crucibles where there is a joining of human need and divine power. The apparent problem is that divine power seems too distant from 21st-century seekers. This, I have discovered, is not true. The power is as present as we are. They are joined, but a way must be

■ ■ ■ ■ ■ ■ ■ ■

found so that the power that has always been destined to be expressed can find its way into the world. It is my hope that *The Gathering* will assist you so that your hopes will not die, but eventually become a faith that knows that with God nothing is impossible!

* * * * * * *

Introduction

The chapters that follow explain in detail the nine steps of a prayer practice called "The Gathering." The practice can be the companion for an individual and become the foundation for a genuine and ever deepening experience of God's presence and power, or a group of explorers can make the steps the center of their prayer lives as they seek not only to live in oneness with God, but also to serve others through the mystery of divine power. Below are the nine steps that are explored in the book.

Step 1 – I release my human need.

Step 2 – I accept my human condition so I can express my spiritual nature.

Step 3 – I willingly release any part of my human self that is a barrier to God.

Step 4 – I willingly forgive others.

Step 5 – I willingly forgive myself. I am precious to God.

that you will discover an approach to life that will open the door of your soul to the kingdom of God.

Step 1

I Release My Human Need.

Most prayer begins with a human need. The need is not put aside; it is presented to God in the hope that God will act, and the body will be healed, the relationship restored, the job acquired or the decision made. The hope is that the need will be resolved to our satisfaction. We have tried to meet the challenge and resolve the problem, but we have failed. Perhaps God will prevail.

Focusing on the need seems reasonable, but what the mind dwells on tends to fill the mind. Obviously, a need is an expression of lack; it is something we do not have, and if we think about what we do not have, the mind is filled with thoughts of lack.

Humanity has discovered that *thoughts held in mind produce after their kind.* Thoughts of lack multiply. Early in the morning, we think about what we do not have and similar thoughts join us during the day and become so numerous that they keep us up at night. Day by day, night by night, the thoughts support one another. What was once thought becomes a belief in limitation. The belief spreads throughout our consciousness, and attitudes are born that become the lens through which we see our lives and the world. Dreams die, and with them the possibility of a meaningful, fulfilled life. For this reason, we must be cautious with our needs and learn the positive role they can play in our lives.

Consider the needs of the human family that cry out for resolution. Famine strikes a large percentage of the earth's population, and nearly 20 million people die of malnutrition and its complications every year, most of them children. The AIDS epidemic is devastating the African continent, killing the greatest natural resource of the region—children. Such calamities are present everywhere, and just as prevalent is the human cry, "Why doesn't God do something about these needs?" The answer is gut-wrenching: a need is not an avenue through which God can work.

What God Can Do

This gut-wrenching fact is obvious. Whatever God is doing, God is always doing it. Spirit does not rest from Its creation. There is no vacation or furlough for God. If God could end the wars that plague the earth, it would be done. If the Almighty could end the pandemics, they would be no more. The hard truth is this: God does not fulfill needs. However, this truth does not mean that needs cannot be met. War can end. Famine can be replaced with plenty, and there is a cure for AIDS and every malady that afflicts the body. Humanity's failure to grasp and understand the preceding ideas has led to disillusionment with God and the perpetuation through the ages of one calamity after another. We continue to insist that a need is an avenue for God's power, and it is not. Rather than insist God work through our needs, it is best for us to discover the avenue through which God's power and presence can be expressed. Before this chapter ends, we will know what the avenue is and what we must do.

Remember, God's labor is not resolving our needs. If God's work was handling needs, when a need appeared, it would be met, but it is obvious that this is not happening. Rather than asking why God doesn't act, it is better for us to discover what God is doing and how we are to act.

Joel Goldsmith, a 20th-century mystic and healer, answered this question best. *What God can do, God is doing*.[1] And what is God doing? God is being; God is being our source, and when we become aware of God as our source, our needs are met. God is being life, and when we experience this life, we are healed. God is being wisdom, and when we experience this light, our path is clear, and wise decisions come easily.

A couple I know both lost their jobs in the same month. They said that in previous years they would have panicked and begun an immediate and desperate search for employment. They would have affirmed perfect employment because employment was the answer to their dilemma.

Facing this challenging situation, they took a different approach. First they paused. There was no panic, for they knew there was inner work for them to do. They understood that employment was not the answer to their challenge; the answer was an awareness of the Source. The need for employment turned them to God, not to ask for employment, but to open themselves to experience God as their Source. They continued to practice the principle of giving and they experienced Spirit as their Source. Now both of them

* * * * * * * *

have jobs that are fulfilling and that abundantly meet their earthly needs. The answer was not two jobs, but the discovery that God was and is their Source.

Needs Serve a Purpose

Needs do serve a purpose; they turn us to God. Nearly every miracle recorded in the Bible began with a need. The widow with the small flask of oil whose sons were about to be sold into slavery to pay her debts experienced an unlimited supply, but the miracle began with her need. Jesus fed 5,000 people with five loaves of bread and two fish, but the miracle began with a need—hungry people. It has always been this way. Needs are not avenues for God's expression, but they do turn us to God. The next step is to turn from the need.

We identify the need and then no longer focus on it. We turn to God and release the need. This brings us closer to discovering the true avenue for God's power, for just as it is obvious that humanity has needs, it is likewise obvious that needs are met, and in some instances through incredible expressions of divine power.

Wick of the Candle

Consider for a moment a candle. During workshop presentations, I sometimes ask two people to join me on stage. I give one person a candle and the other a box of matches. I ask that the candle be lit. Then I hold another candle, and ask that it, too, be lit. A match is struck, and the person with the matches attempts to light my candle; however, he will fail.

I ask, "Is there a problem?" Eventually, the person trying to light the candle notices that my candle has no wick. "There is no wick," he says. "Is that a problem?" I reply. "Yes," he answers.

A candle without a wick is a problem. I point out to the audience that the candle contains enough fuel to produce light and warmth for hours, but we cannot access them because there is no wick. This is the truth in God's kingdom. All we need exists close at hand. All the love we will ever need rests within us, for God has made a home in us. If we need wisdom, supply, peace or strength, it is within our grasp. It is closer than breath, but a wick is required.

You, dear friend, were created to be a wick in God's candle. You might think a person is a wick, but this is not true. The wick is actually a person *who is aware of God's presence*. The steps of The Gathering prepare us to become an avenue for God's expression. We will be blessed, but we will also become avenues through which others can be blessed as well.

Remember the role of the need: to turn us to God. Through the need, God is calling you. There are powerful principles that govern this aspect of our lives. Today we have discovered that needs are not avenues for God's expression. We know that God cannot act through a need, but that when we become aware of God's presence, we are wicks in the candle. It is then that miracles can happen.

One More Principle

Step 1 of The Gathering reveals another principle: "Your Father knows what you need before you ask him" (Mt. 6:8). Most people are relieved to know that God knows what they lack and what they need, that they need to be healed or that they need a job. This is the general understanding of Jesus' statement. We think God is so wise that He knows our problems. There are other possible interpretations and other questions that come to mind when the statement *God knows our need before we ask* is examined in depth.

Is there a need to ask God for anything when God already knows what we need? Certainly we are not supplying God with new information. Perhaps the

. . . .

asking is for us. Perhaps it opens us to receive. Maybe there is a need we have that Spirit is aware of, but we are not. Another bizarre possibility is that Spirit is unaware of our needs.

In Habakkuk 1:13, it is written, "Your eyes are too pure to behold evil." Is it possible that God's eyes are too pure to behold our need? Certainly it is true that there are no needs in God. When a person experiences the Presence, there is no lack, there is no disease, and there is no conflict.

In *How I Used Truth*, H. Emilie Cady writes of immersing herself in the "very highest statement of truth that I could formulate. *There is only God; all else is a lie.*"[2] She had faced days of excruciating pain from a badly sprained ankle. As she gave herself to this spiritual practice, the lie, the sprained ankle, disappeared. It was healed because Cady entered a state of mind and heart where there was only God; there was no sprained ankle. This is the consciousness that awaits us. The steps of The Gathering prepare us for this experience.

As these ideas race through my mind, I am aware that the one central need in my life is to know God. This, I believe, is the need of which Jesus spoke. Spirit knows we need to be aware of It. When this awareness occurs, Spirit has an avenue through which to do Its work.

There are no needs in God, so I must not bring a need to the Creator. However, I experience needs, and they have a role to play in my life. They turn me to God. Once the turn begins, I leave the need behind and bring only myself to the Creator, as well as my deep desire to experience all that God is. This is the first step of The Gathering. It asks you to release your human need and to bring instead yourself and a desire to awaken to the presence of God.

Taking the Step

If you are using The Gathering for your personal prayer practice, you need only speak or think the words of Step 1: *I release my human need*. Sometimes it is good to be specific about the need you are releasing. For instance, *I release my human need for employment* or *I release my human need to be healed*. This surrender may be difficult, but I encourage you to do it. Remember, humanity has brought needs to God for thousands of years with little success. It is time to try something new.

Step 2

I Accept My Human Condition So I Can Express My Spiritual Nature.

Nonresistance

It seemed impractical for the first step in the resolution of our challenges to be the releasing of our human needs, but this is what we have done, and we have done it willingly, with a realistic hope that we have done the right thing. The second step of The Gathering is just as implausible as the first, but it, too, promises to bring us closer not only to a solution to the problem, but also closer to the One who gives us breath.

Most of us have no intention of accepting pain, anguish or weaknesses; we want to be rid of them. To accept such feelings and limitations would be to admit defeat and condemn ourselves to a life unworthy of our true nature. Acceptance, we think, is self-effacing and the way of the weak. Notice, however, the implication of Step 2—acceptance of the condition in some way contributes to the expression of our spiritual nature. Could it be that the true challenge is not to rid ourselves of a human condition, but to express who and what we are? Could it be that human conditions and challenges lose their power and even disappear when our spiritual nature appears?

How many times have we confronted a problem with our best efforts only to find that not only does it remain in place, it also seems to grow stronger? We have resisted the situation and discovered that as we wrestled with the problem, our grip on it tightened. The hand on our throat was our own. We expected freedom and found we were imprisoned by our own noble, yet misguided attempts to solve the problem. We are more bound and restricted and in pain today than the previous day.

In Step 2, *I accept my human condition so that I can express my spiritual nature* is a statement of nonresistance. As we take this step, we are closer to one of the grandest experiences of our lives, a spiritual breakthrough that makes all things possible.

* * * * * * *

Fully Human

Acceptance of one's human condition may at first create more inner turmoil than the impact of the condition itself. The "natural" impulse is to act, and acceptance asks us to wait and to not resist. This is challenging, but there is a form of acceptance that is even more daunting—acceptance of our human selves.

Many years ago, during a time of prayer and meditation, the following words filled my mind: *Unless you are willing to accept your humanity, you will not be able to express your divinity.* Acceptance is most challenging when it is brought to bear on ourselves. Most of us either try to war against our humanity or run from it. It is the primitive response of our ancient selves. Our flight can take the form of hiding our frailties and weaknesses from others and ourselves. We try to push aside hurtful memories and feelings only to have them ambush us later, at a time when we are little prepared for such a confrontation.

During the time in my life when I was trying to understand the insight that came to me, I conducted a weekend spiritual retreat with a group of friends from around the world. The first night I tried my best to talk about self-acceptance. At the conclusion of my remarks, I stepped forward and said, "Will you

▪ ▪ ▪ ▪ ▪ ▪ ▪

accept me just the way I am?" In unison, the group responded, "We accept you just the way you are." It was a powerful experience of unconditional love.

I then asked each person in turn to come and light a candle, stand before the group, and ask to be accepted unconditionally. Again and again the words were spoken, "Will you accept me just the way I am?" and with each question came the loving response, "We accept you just the way you are."

This simple ceremony set the tone for the retreat. It was one of the most loving experiences of my life. In fact, throughout the retreat, when a person would admit to some inappropriate act from the past, someone would invariably say, "We accept you just the way you are." Everyone would laugh, but the one sharing the depth of his or her soul would feel cherished and loved by those present.

There comes a time on our spiritual journey when we realize that the answer to any difficulty is to express ourselves as the unlimited spiritual beings we are. We become willing to discover ourselves as children of God. We think that by giving attention to this aspect of our being we can avoid experiencing our human selves. This is not true. Not only must we accept and become nonresistant to conditions, we must become accepting of and nonresistant to those parts of ourselves we have tried to conceal. We hide them deep inside, hoping no one will see them, but isn't it interesting that what we try to hide within us stands in the open for all to see? We think our insecurity is hidden, but those around us know our bravado is a not-so-elaborate disguise of a wounded soul.

This form of acceptance is not the way of the weak, but the way of the one who is willing to love fearlessly. Acceptance is nonresistance in action, and love's first expression. Have you noticed that those who love you unconditionally accept you as you are—warts and all?

Many years ago a woman came to me for counseling. She wanted to approach weight loss from a spiritual perspective. She shared her feelings and struggles with losing weight. I listened and because I was beginning to work with the power of acceptance, I said to her, "It doesn't really matter whether you lose the weight or gain another 10 pounds. The work is to remember that you are a spiritual being, a child of God." We prayed together and she left. Not long after our conversation, I left the ministry where I was serving, and I lost track of the woman. A year later she contacted me and told me that she had lost nearly 80 pounds. I invited her to come by my office, and we shared a meal at the Unity Inn. During our time together she told me what had happened the day of the counseling appointment.

She said that when I told her the weight was not the real issue but rather the discovery of her true nature, she felt accepted. Basically I accepted her as she was. This was important because it enabled her to accept herself as she was. Not until she accepted her condition could she take steps to lose the weight.

This is the heart of Step 2. Acceptance is an expression of our spiritual nature. It is evidence that the human condition is being met. Step 2 does not ignore human problems, nor our frailties and weaknesses. The step acknowledges our failings and assigns a proper place for them. Moreover, it presents Spirit's great gift of love to the challenging parts of our human selves..

Love Yourself

Step 2 asks us to love ourselves, and as love does its work, fear is cast out. No longer do we fear our past, our memories or feelings associated with what has gone before. Our thoughts are harmonized, and we eventually see the events of the past differently. The second step asks us to be fully alive, to fully embrace life.

■ ■ ■ ■ ■ ■ ■ ■

Events trouble us, but the fear of lacking the wisdom, strength or courage to face such events troubles us most. It is not past memories, but guilt originating in the past that plagues us today. To embrace life is to allow ourselves to experience our memories, thoughts and feelings.

In our society, men have difficulty with their feelings. We tend to shun them and hold emotions at bay. People who know me today are shocked to learn that I once behaved as the typical male. The breakthrough began at ministerial school after serving in the Navy. I had been a naval aviator flying more than 100 combat missions over North Vietnam when I entered my spiritual training.

I remember sitting in a prayer service and feeling deeply moved. I could feel the pressure of tears and struggled to hold them inside. I failed to do so and the tears flowed down my face. I also burst a blood vessel in my left eye. I was having a spiritual experience and resisting it. The pressure on many levels was more than I could bear. I was coming to life and saying no to the activity of God.

I learned from the experience and began to allow the tears to flow easily. Having come from a military family and environment, I was embarrassed at first, but I eventually accepted the movement of Spirit

. . . .

within me. For a time, the pendulum swung from no emotions to dripping with emotion, but the balance did come. Now I am fully alive. I cry, I feel, I am alive, but the beginning was acceptance.

There is a hunger in us for love's great gift of acceptance. We may think we want the memories, thoughts and feelings they evoke to go away, but what we really want is to be loved the way we are. Acceptance allows us to pull back the covers and look again at what we have hidden. There will be no attempt to chastise or destroy what we have tried to put aside. Nothing is shunned or resisted, for to resist our humanity is to resist God. Resistance to God is a lack of faith in the power of divine love and acceptance.

We tend to think that loving ourselves is something we do, but it is actually God's work, and it is work that God naturally does, for God is love. Here is a prayer practice that makes Step 2 real. Here is an easy question for you. If you had to face a difficult situation such as testifying in court, would you rather go by yourself or have your best friend at your side even though your friend would have to remain silent during the proceedings? The answer is obvious; you would want your friend at your side.

■ ■ ■ ■ ■ ■ ■ ■

Now consider the following prayer practice. You begin by turning your attention to Spirit. You ask only to experience God. You might affirm the following ideas: *I am not alone. All the wisdom, love, strength and peace are with me, for these dear friends are the essence of my being. There is nothing to fear, for I am a child of God. No earthly thing, no thought, no feeling or image has power over me, for God is at work in my life.* You affirm such ideas and then wait for Spirit's confirmation that the ideas held in your mind are true. If your mind drifts to the past or future, you bring it home again with a simple idea, such as *I have nothing to fear; God is at work in my life.*

Once you have a sense of God's presence, you then bring to mind an image or memory that you have wanted to forget. To recall the memory is to evoke thoughts and feelings you have wanted to deny, push aside or bury inside. Now they are rising up in you, but today there is a difference. Now they are rising into a consciousness of God's presence, where there is only the power of God. Fear has no power where there is love. Anger dissolves in God's peace. Guilt cannot live where there is acceptance.

Can you see that this prayer practice is quite different from what usually happens when unwanted feelings and thoughts rise up in consciousness?

Typically the feelings ambush us, demean us and then retreat again into the hiding place we have prepared for them.

This prayer practice places you in control as you call the memories, thoughts and feelings front and center where you may experience them, but they are also rising into a consciousness of love where they have no power, where they dissolve. Repeated use of this prayer practice enables us to discover through experience that acceptance of our humanity is a prelude to the expression of our authentic selves. I have used this practice many times. I have shared it with other people, and so now it is yours to put to the test, but this is not the only practice I would suggest to you.

The Banquet

Picture in your mind a banquet. You have invited all aspects of your self. Guilt and shame are present. Your insecurity and anger are in attendance. Hurtful memories have joined the party. At the appointed time, you stand and welcome your innermost thoughts, feelings and memories. You invite each to stand and speak. As guilt rises, you stand by its side and gently place your arm on its shoulder or around its waist. Guilt pours forth its story. Tears flow. After guilt has finished speaking, you simply say, *Thank you for being here. Thank you for standing and speaking.*

Notice there is no judgment of what has been said. You do not contend with guilt or justify behavior or actions. Your role is acceptance, and it is healing. Obviously this meditative practice takes time and commitment, but it works. Every part of you that has been shunned can be asked to "stand and speak" as you stand at its side.

I trust you can now see the promise of Step 2. Acceptance of our human selves places us in a state of nonresistance that allows for the expression of our spiritual nature. It takes years for a person to realize that nonacceptance of our humanity is a barrier to God. Resistance of any kind in the soul is resistance to God. Nonresistance invites Spirit's expression and calls for us to live as the spiritual beings we truly are.

· · · · · · · ·

secure life, but we are unaware of the treasure so close to us.

The problem does not lie with God; it rests with us. Our attention is fixed on the world our five senses make known to us, but there is more to experience than our senses can reveal. There are attitudes and beliefs we reaffirm each day by the way we live our lives that do not work for us or contribute to the life we want to live. If we live in limitation, it is not because Spirit is withholding Itself or Its gifts from us, but because we shield ourselves from the possibilities of what can be. We adopt attitudes and beliefs that we think protect us and move us forward in life, but they do not.

One of the most effective programs for inner transformation is the 12 steps of Alcoholics Anonymous. Step by step a person is guided toward a potential spiritual awakening. The participants are asked to make a fearless moral inventory of themselves and thereby become conscious of the barriers that stand between the person and not only sobriety, but also spiritual awakening. Step 6 of the AA program finds the individual ready to have the defects of character removed.

Every spiritual practice encourages the release of the barriers that stand between us and the life we are

▪ ▪ ▪ ▪ ▪ ▪ ▪ ▪

destined to live. The challenge is that often we are unaware of the walls we have erected. We may even believe the barrier is a blessing. It is a fence to prevent harm when in fact it stifles our full expression as caring, loving people.

Consider the following situation that tends to repeat itself after every divorce. There is emotional pain, often deep and intense. One or both of the individuals determine that they will never experience such pain again. In that moment of self-determination, a foundation is laid for a wall that has the noble purpose of protecting the person from the pain that is so acute. The problem with walls is that they may be good at keeping others out, but they also hem us in. The person goes forward in life wanting a loving relationship, but wondering why the right person has not appeared or why one relationship after another begins with promise but ends as quickly as it began. Imagine the ongoing pain present in the United States, where almost 50 percent of marriages end in divorce. After any traumatic experience, it is a normal human tendency to want to protect ourselves, but there is a better way.

Willingness is the beginning of nearly every new endeavor. We may not know the solution to a problem, but we can be willing to discover the answer. We may not know what to do, but we can be willing to act. Willingness generates hope and opens the mind, and a hopeful, open mind is an avenue for the activity of Spirit. In this instance, we are declaring our willingness to release any part of our human self that is a barrier to God. Attitudes and beliefs can be the culprits, and feelings such as guilt and shame are as restrictive as prison bars.

One of the foundation pillars of The Gathering prayer practice is acceptance. We put acceptance to the test in Step 2 when we accepted our human conditions. Now *release* is our watchword as we sever the bond we forged with those things that serve as a barrier to God.

As we master Step 3, we join people of ancient times who also discovered the power of letting go. They called it sacrifice, but at the heart of sacrifice is a willingness to let go and release anything that is a barrier to God. An offering of grain or a lamb may be made, but it is our desire to hold on, because of our fear of tomorrow, that is the true culprit. In sacrifice or letting go, the willingness to put God first opens our souls to receive.

While in prayer and meditation once, a thought entered my mind. Actually it was a phrase: *no longer holding on, allowing myself to be held*. We hold on to so much—feelings, beliefs that don't work, people and the past. Everlasting arms await us if we will let go.

Currently I live in Fort Myers, Florida. Prior to moving to Florida, my wife and I had built what we thought was our retirement home in Lake of the Ozarks, Missouri. We even named our house on the bluff overlooking the lake. We built some of it with our own hands and had even created a three-story observatory named after the house, which we called The High Meadow. I remember it was when the colors of autumn glorified God that guidance started to creep into my mind: *it's time to go.* I quickly dismissed the thought, but it kept returning. In December, I talked to Nancy about a potential move, and she was shocked. She said she would drive into our driveway and weep. Obviously neither one of us was allowing ourselves to be held. We were holding on.

Eventually circumstances arose that made it evident that a move was in order. After living at The High Meadow full-time for five years and having enjoyed it for more than 14 years, we surrendered to the guidance, let go of past dreams, and left a place where we thought we would always live. Now we know you can let go of the good for a greater good.

Not every one is so fortunate to release one form of good for another. At times, what we cling to is now

* ∎ ∎ ∎ ∎ ∎ ∎ ∎

rooted in us and taking on a life of its own. Guilt, regret and resentment become familiar companions, and we have no life without them. It is time to let go, but how? The answer may be to remember that sacrifice or letting go has a purpose. It is one step on a journey to experience the Presence of God.

The Tabernacle

The roots of Step 3 are ancient. The structure of the Jewish tabernacle, the forerunner of the Temple, tells us much about our spiritual journey. There was a single entrance to the structure symbolizing a single-mindedness and pure desire to know and experience God, for Spirit was in the midst of the tabernacle, in the Holy of Holies.

The trailhead of the spiritual path is littered with people wanting God to do their bidding. They either want Spirit to fulfill their human needs, or they desire the gifts God can give rather than Spirit Itself. And so we stand at the entrance of the tabernacle, the trailhead of the spiritual journey, affirm our desire for God, and step into the outer courtyard to find ourselves standing before an altar where offerings are made and sacrifices are burnt.

The message is powerful and clear: We proclaim we desire only God. However, God is asking us,

"What are you willing to release?" This is where we are now, standing before the altar and discovering that a spiritual life is not addition, but subtraction.

The masterpiece is in the stone, for the Master Mason has crafted our true self; but now through subtraction, chips of stone, rigid thoughts and beliefs, feelings of guilt, shame and insecurity are cast aside, and slowly the masterpiece is revealed.

Pause and you will hear Spirit asking, "What are you willing to release? What do you need to sacrifice so that you can move forward in your spiritual journey? What burden do you need to let go of before you can soar?"

. . . .

Taking the Step

If you are using The Gathering for your personal prayer practice, you need only speak or think the words of Step 3: *I willingly release any part of my human self that is a barrier to God.* It is suggested that you pause and listen to Spirit speaking to you, as if it were asking, "What are you willing to release? What do you need to sacrifice, so you can move forward in your spiritual journey? What burden do you need to let go of before you can soar?" Take the step and listen as answers come from within you, for there is a part of you that knows the answers to the questions above.

If you are using The Gathering as a group prayer practice, each person speaks Step 3 out loud. There is no discussion as each person speaks. Once the statement is spoken by each member, The Gathering continues to Step 4.

Step 4

I Willingly Forgive Others.

A Great Barrier

One of the great barriers to an experience of God's presence is lack of forgiveness. We justify our anger, and it becomes resentment, and if it is fed long enough by hurtful memories, thoughts of revenge and behavior, it grows into hatred, and a hate-filled soul cannot feel God's love. We may strike out at the other person, but our hands are around our own throat, restricting our ability to breathe peace and harmony into our world. We limit ourselves with our lack of forgiveness of others, but it is also possible to be unwilling to forgive ourselves. This chapter challenges us to forgive those we believe have harmed us.

Presence symbolized by the altar and remember that we have something against another, we are to resolve the issue and then approach the altar again. In a conversation between Jesus and his disciple Peter, it was asked how often shall we do this? How often shall we forgive another person? "Lord, if another member of the church sins against me, how often should I forgive? As many as seven times?" Jesus said to him, "Not seven times, but, I tell you, seventy-seven times" (Mt. 18:21-22). It is obvious from Jesus' answer that forgiveness is not for the other person; it is for us, and now we know why—because it is a barrier to an awareness of God.

We live this verse of Scripture again and again. We think an issue is resolved. The negative feelings subside. A breath is taken, and we assure ourselves that all is well. The crisis is behind us, we have moved beyond it. And then it happens: the ex-spouse can't take our child on the weekend we are going out of town with a friend, and he refuses to change his newly formed plans. He doesn't like that we are seeing someone and that the relationship is about to rise to another level. The rage returns, and we begin to believe we will need all of the 490 opportunities to forgive that Jesus referred to when speaking to Peter.

■　■　■　■　■　■　■　■

Enemies Are of Our Household

Few of us have feelings toward another person that are so intense we call the individual our enemy, but perhaps we must expand our understanding of the nature of the "enemy." Jesus said that our enemies are of our own household. A literal view of his statement seems to indicate that he is referring to family members, and certainly there are conflicts in some households, but his insight is more far-reaching, for it touches all of us.

It is we who hold resentments, and therefore the work of forgiveness is ours to do. We may blame our feelings on another person, but feelings are not in the other individual or in the great divide between us; they are literally within us. They are of our household. The conflict is not between two people; the conflict is in us. We are at war with our true nature. There is no resolution to the conflict until peace reigns in our souls, and we are expressing our loving self. Forgiveness is then reduced to a simple idea; it is a return to love.

Returning to Love

Here is a three-step process that can help release love from within you. First, write a catharsis letter to the person you dislike. Get those feelings out so you can see them, so you can feel them. Release the venom that has limited and poisoned your life, but don't mail the letter! Write it, wait three days, reread it, and then ceremoniously burn it. I have known people who built a simple altar upon which to burn the letter.

Second, write a blessing letter for a newborn child. Bless this new citizen of our planet with all the wisdom, strength, creativity, goodness and joy you can imagine. Write the letter and then change the salutation to the name of the person who challenges you. Read the letter each morning and each night for 40 days. This practice prepares you for the third and final step.

Send an anonymous gift to the person who has been the object of your consternation. The individual must never know it came from you. This practice will transform you. When you share an anonymous gift, you activate the law of giving and receiving. The law must be fulfilled, but in this instance, no one can satisfy the law because no one knows you gave the gift. Therefore God must fulfill the law, and the only gift Spirit can give is Itself. The result is growth in consciousness. An awareness of God as love fills your being. Through grace you have found your way home again; you have returned to love.

Anonymous giving blesses the giver, but it also causes the recipient of the gift to look differently at the world. Suddenly the person finds him/herself living in a friendly universe. He looks around and wonders who gave the gift. Was it a co-worker or a relative? Possibilities abound and the mystery brings a smile to his face.

It has been my privilege to assist people with the third step in returning to love. I have taken cards and gifts with me during my travels and mailed them. There was even a class of individuals who sent me their anonymous gifts, and I mailed them from a remote location. Imagine a person receiving a gift from an unknown person postmarked from a place likewise unknown to them.

. . . .

Taking the Step

If you are using The Gathering for your personal prayer practice, speak or think the words of Step 4: *I willingly forgive others*. Rest in the silence with this statement of intent and then write your two letters, one to release your feelings and the other to bless the one you resent. The letters will help to open your heart, so you can send your anonymous gift and return to love.

If you are using The Gathering as a group prayer practice, each person speaks Step 4 out loud. There is no discussion as each person speaks. Once the statement is spoken by each member, The Gathering continues to Step 5.

Step 5

I Willingly Forgive Myself.
I Am Precious to God.

The Echo

Forgiving others is difficult, but the greater challenge is forgiving ourselves, and so we take another step. *I willingly forgive myself. I am precious to God.* As before, willingness is the beginning. We may not be able to forgive ourselves, but we are willing to believe forgiveness is possible; we are willing to consider that in spite of what we have done, left undone, and what has been done to us, we are worthy of love.

Why are we so hard on ourselves? Is it because of our actions? Could we have written these words the apostle Paul wrote: "For I do not do what I want, but I do the very thing I hate" (Rom. 7:15 RSV)? Are we hard on ourselves because we believe we are what we do, or because we believe what other people say about us, or because we believe what we say about ourselves?

It seems obvious that what a person says about us cannot change us. The actual words have no lasting effect; it is the echo that does the damage. The echo is the words we say to ourselves about ourselves. Long ago, an authority figure may have expressed an opinion about us with the question, "What's wrong with you?" We heard the statement behind the question (something was wrong with us) and we adopted this statement as our own. The words became a belief that we were broken. Through the years, we echoed the words of long ago and began to act as though we were in need of repair. Our relationships suffered because of the unconscious belief that a broken person is not wanted or needed by another. The self-loathing grew, and we now feel guilt that seems to have no specific origin—a guilt, like most guilt, that demands punishment. We have done nothing that warrants lawful retribution, so we punish ourselves with limitation. We say no to success.

I once knew a nurse who had made a mistake that injured one of her patients. Because of her actions, she stepped away from a profession she loved. Years later she yearned to return to nursing and began to take the required courses to become recertified. Her class work and practicum were excellent. There was no way she could fail—unless she failed to take the final exam. Her lack of self-forgiveness for a past omission asserted itself again, and she was not present for the exam.

A day later she was in my office. She told me her story, and I understood what she had done and why she had done it. It was time for a breakthrough, for her to realize that she was precious to God. The pattern could be broken if she took the test. I suggested she talk to her instructor and ask to take a makeup exam. She made the request; it was accepted, and she easily passed the final exam and once again became a loving, caring nurse.

The Mark of Cain

We all make mistakes, yet none are so grievous that they alter God's nature. There is nothing we can do or fail to do that can cause God to stop loving us. This truth was illustrated long ago through the story of Cain and Abel.

Adam and Eve had two sons. The elder, Cain, slew his younger brother, Abel, and feared for his life. He knew the law: an eye for an eye and a tooth for a tooth. Curiously, God put a mark on Cain that preserved his life. Why was he protected? He murdered his brother. Why not let him die at the hand of another, an enactment of the law of retribution?

Perhaps the mark was placed on Cain because he was precious to God. If God did not value him, there would have been no mark, and he would have perished. I have wondered about the mark of Cain. What kind of mark was it? Did it carry a message to those who saw it?

Many years ago in prayer and meditation, an answer came to me. I thought of Cain banished from his land, a wanderer begging for food. Looking forlorn, he came to a door holding in his outstretched hand his begging bowl. The person answering the door saw him and at first frowned, but then she saw the mark, a mark that declared to all who saw it that the one who bore it was precious to God. A smile crossed the face of Cain's new hostess, and he was warmly received and fed.

Cain must have been puzzled. He had murdered his brother. Why was he treated with respect? He may have thought he deserved to die, or at least to be treated with disdain. As he wandered, I wondered how long it took him to realize he was precious to God. This was his real problem; he did not believe he had divine worth. How many of us fail to realize that we have sacred worth, that we all bear the mark of Cain, for we are all precious to God?

Who Is on the Phone?

Remember the echo—the inner voice, the voice of our human self that whispers its lies in our inner ear? It tells us what we cannot do. It reminds us of past failures. It says we're not very smart, we don't deserve happiness because of what we have done or because of what has been done to us.

When we hear this voice, let us measure its content against what God is perpetually saying to us. Spirit sings a chorus in our souls: *You are precious to me. You are my beloved.* If the thoughts filling our minds do not support these two statements, they are lies.

Dear friend, we must discern who is on the phone. Is it possible for the voice that says we are precious and beloved to call us worthless and an utter failure as well? Is it possible? Certainly not!

The problem is that we do not know what we are. We think we are flesh and blood. We think we are what we do, what has been done to us, what others say to us or what we say to ourselves. The question is "What does Spirit see when It looks at us?" The

* * * * * * *

answer: an image of Itself, precious, loved and cherished.

How Powerful Are We?

How powerful are we? Water seeks its own level. This is an expression of its nature. Can we alter this quality of water? Can we, by thought or intention, make the water forget its disposition to seek a common level? How powerful are we? Can we alter the natural inclination of a seed to sprout and grow into a mature plant bearing fruit and more seeds? Can we change what God has made? If God is love, and love is God's nature, is there anything we can do to stop God from loving us? Just how powerful are we?

In matters of the heart, God's heart, we have no power. Love does what love does, and no thought, word or human deed can alter the nature of the Divine. However, as we have discovered, it is possible for us to erect a barrier that clouds our vision and hardens our hearts, so we cannot feel the perpetual love of God. We are precious to God, but our unwillingness to forgive ourselves for transgressions committed or imagined wrongs limits our ability to live and experience life as it is meant to be.

In rational moments, even the person filled with resentment and hate knows that the feelings held

* * * * * * *

inside foul the nest. We intuitively know that forgiveness of ourselves will open doors to a new expression of our nature, but the question is "How do we forgive ourselves?" This may be one of the most important discoveries of our lives. This one discovery creates more freedom than all the wars of liberation. We may strike out at one another, but the heaviest blows are self-inflicted.

Steps to Self-Forgiveness

The path to healing is feeling, and the first step to freedom from guilt and self-loathing is the most difficult part of the journey. It takes courage and just the hint of understanding that we are not our feelings. As it is with all things spiritual, God is the beginning. Remember the ancient alpha: "In the beginning God." We turn our attention to God, open our mind and heart, and let our human desires for many things be replaced by the simplicity of our innate yearning for our Creator. Let us pause in prayer and meditation and ask for one thing, the only thing a person with a single eye would desire—God and then be still as grace grants us an experience of the Presence. While in this peaceful state, we bring to mind memories that generate the guilt we so detest. (Remember, the path to healing is feeling, and only the courageous can be free.)

As we recall the events of the past, our memories become a path for the feelings we have wanted to avoid. Let the thoughts and feelings meet the Presence of God that fills our consciousness because of our time of prayer and meditation.

What is more real and enduring—the Presence of God or the feelings of fear and guilt? Bring the darkness of your feelings into the light of God and watch. Suddenly there is no darkness, only God. This practice reveals the power of prayer and meditation, the power of a consciousness of God to heal all things.

This spiritual practice is to be tested. Anger and its more enduring companion, resentment, are often a part of our lives. Many of us experience some anger on a regular basis. This is an opportunity to test the prayer and meditation practice above.

On a day when you have experienced anger, pause and step aside as soon as you can. A self-imposed "time-out" is a good idea. Give attention to God and open yourself to Spirit. In this Presence, there is no anger or resentment; there is peace and love. When you sense the peace, revel in it for a time, and then recall the event that seemed to generate the anger. The memory will bring anger and resentment

■ ■ ■ ■ ■ ■ ■ ■

into your current state of consciousness, the peace of God, and you will discover that these feelings have no power here. How could they? Instead the anger and resentment dissolve, and you find the peace that is your true nature.

Consider for a moment the image of a hurt child. If we saw a child in pain, what would we do? Would we push the child away as we have shoved away our feelings of hurt, fear, anger and guilt? No, every hurt child is to be embraced. We kneel with outstretched arms to become a haven of comfort for the little one.

Let us be such a safe harbor for our feelings. Only by allowing ourselves to experience our emotions can we be free. Instead of trying to avoid the feelings, we experience and then accept them.

Acceptance is the beginning of love. When love is just beginning, it does not contend with but rather accepts our humanity. This is what we must do with our feelings.

When Two Become One

Consider how the image of the hurt child can help us forgive ourselves. Rest in prayer and meditation, and let the image form in the mind. As we look closely, we see that the child is us many years ago. We stretch out our arms and welcome this little one into our heart. Observe the child's reluctance. Meet this timidity with a smile of understanding as we continue to care for the one we once were. Watch carefully as he or she moves slowly forward, closer to our arms. We feel the child's arms encircle us as our arms encircle the child. Hold on tight, but gently, and notice the merger of the hurt child we used to be and the adult we are today. In these moments of oneness, the past loses it power and we are healed. No longer do we shun the past. Past and present join, and we become whole again, whole as we have always been.

Prayer practices and visualization help us return to love as we forgive ourselves, but the day must come when we take action in the world. We do what no guilty person would ever do. We do something *nice* for ourselves. As long as guilt persists, we will limit, if not unconsciously punish, ourselves. As we forgive ourselves, we treat ourselves with respect, and our inner conversations support and lift us rather than tear us down.

Kindness shared with self can take many forms. A massage is a good way to pamper ourselves as well as a trip to a favorite shop. In my Florida community, pastry chef Norman Love is a world famous chocolatier. His chocolate is for special occasions, and there is nothing more special that learning to forgive ourselves. A bite of chocolate cannot heal the soul, but our willingness to treat ourselves to a small confection might be a first step toward treating ourselves with respect.

It is strange, but those who do not forgive themselves are self-absorbed. They share no random acts of kindness and fail to reach out to others, not because they do not want to or because they do not believe in the need to serve others, but because their thoughts are not about others: they are about themselves. Those who forgive themselves realize they are precious to God. They live in a world much larger than their past guilt and pain.

Forgiveness rests in discovering who we are. We are not the things we have done or left undone, said or not said. We are spiritual beings, children of God, loved and precious to the Creator.

Taking the Step

If you are using The Gathering for your personal prayer practice, speak or think the words of Step 5: *I willingly forgive myself. I am precious to God.* Rest in the silence with this statement of intent and put to the test some of the practices offered above.

If you are using The Gathering as a group prayer practice, each person speaks Step 5 out loud. There is no discussion as each person speaks. Once the statement is spoken by each member, The Gathering continues to Step 6.

Step 6

I Acknowledge That a Consciousness of God Is the Answer ... That Life Is a Consciousness of God.

Life Is a Consciousness of God

Emmet Fox, a 20th-century metaphysician, coined the phrase "life is consciousness." This statement points to a key insight necessary for successful and dynamic living—there is a relationship between our thoughts, attitudes, beliefs and life experiences. If we think we are failures, we tend to fail. Even when victory is in our grasp, we falter. People who carry guilt in their hearts tend to find a way to punish themselves. People who think of themselves as victims can usually point to happenings that substantiate their belief.

* * * * * * *

Our consciousness not only attracts to us like experiences, it also creates the glass through which we see ourselves, others and the world. We don't see the world as it is, but as we are. This is why two different people can view the same situation and draw opposing conclusions. Fox's statement requires in-depth study and daily application. My exploration of both his statement and various prayer practices and their effect on my life has spawned a related statement that is at the heart of The Gathering: *Life is a consciousness of God*.

I have come to believe that experience is consciousness, but life as it is meant to be requires that I become aware or conscious of God. Life is what happens when we become aware of the Presence. In other words, to be alive is to be aware of Spirit.

Being alive is more than drawing breath. It is being conscious of the Presence of God in which we live and move and have our being. Life is not circumstance. Is war life? Is rape or child abuse life? They are certainly not life as it is meant to be. War, rape and child abuse are human experiences, but they are not our destiny, and they are not of God.

The Answer to Prayer

Typically there are numerous answers to prayer. The body is healed, a job is obtained, decisions are made, and relationships are restored, but are these things what God offers us? As human beings, it is natural to want our human needs met. For thousands of years, answered prayer, when it occurred, could be pointed to in the world.

It is true; our problems can be solved. However, let us lay a firm foundation for a new kind of life, one that challenges us to accept the gift of God that is being offered to us. Remember the assurance made in the Gospel of Luke: "It is your Father's good pleasure to give you the kingdom" (Lk. 12:32).

Our narrow, limiting focus is finding a solution to our problem when Spirit is offering Itself to us. If we accepted this gift, would it be enough? If God were real for us, would there be any challenge we could not face? Jesus promised that if we sought the kingdom, all else would be added to us. In other words, if we accept the gift of God that is the Father's good pleasure to give us, our problems will be solved or they will loosen their grip upon us. The gift of God is so great that the solutions we seek in the world are to be viewed as added things.

. . . .

The answered prayer of The Gathering is singular—a consciousness of the One. It is during The Gathering that we either experience Spirit giving Itself to us or lay the foundation for this sacred experience in the near future. Is this consciousness enough, or do we need more? What else could we desire?

This is a challenging way of life. When we are in pain, whether it is of the body or the soul, we want immediate relief. When the value of our assets plummet, our savings are shrinking, and we have lost our job, it is normal to want a swift resolution to the problem. We are concerned about tomorrow, and therefore the promise of peace in the moment is replaced by a fear of the future.

It is in these moments that we have a choice. We can seek to truly come alive or seek again, as we have many times before, to have our earthly needs fulfilled. If we choose to seek the kingdom, an awareness of the Presence of God, we come alive, and what is needed for earthly living is added to us. This is the promise Jesus made: "But seek first the kingdom of God ... and all these things shall be added to you" (Mt. 6:33 NKJV). If we seek the resolution of the problem, an answer may come, but we assure ourselves of another opportunity to choose the kingdom again.

■ ■ ■ ■ ■ ■ ■

Life is more than solving problems; it is an ever-deepening consciousness of our spiritual nature. Let us set our sights on this lofty summit.

I have lived my life this way for decades. It was not easy because the needs I have faced and still face, like those before you, can seem so compelling. For instance, what if there is a financial crisis, an unexpected bill or a devastating loss that current bank accounts cannot cover? When we know the answer to the challenge is a consciousness of the Presence of God, we take our eyes off the problem and turn to Spirit. In fact, as we have seen previously, the need actually turns us to Spirit. We do not know how a consciousness of God as our Source will manifest Itself in our lives, but it will. First there will be peace, and if we remain sensitive to the movement of God within us, we will become aware of ideas and guidance that take us one step closer to the tangible resolution of the problem.

The answer is always the same, an experience of the Presence. God becomes real for us, and then this consciousness allows us to see what we have not seen before, a way through. Along with the sought-for idea and guidance, there comes the strength, persistence and courage to act with boldness and daring until the earthly needs are met.

* * * * * * *

In The Gathering, we don't bring our problems or needs to God; we bring ourselves and our willingness to awaken, and Spirit answers our willingness by giving Itself to us! There is no greater gift.

We have a choice. We can allow a mundane state of consciousness to manifest itself and become our experience, or we can allow a consciousness of Spirit to become our life. Which state of mind and heart promises security, peace and love? The answer is both. Both states of consciousness promise us the joys of life, but only a consciousness of Spirit can grant this gift. First we must identify the value and beauty of what is being offered to us. Once we say yes to God, we awaken in another world, a world that has always been present, waiting for our eyes to see.

Taking the Step

If you are using The Gathering for your personal prayer practice, you need only speak or think the words of Step 6: *I acknowledge that a consciousness of God is the answer ... that life is a consciousness of God.*

If you are using The Gathering as a group prayer practice, the group leader asks everyone to audibly affirm Step 6 in unison. The six steps prepare the individual or the group for the heart of The Gathering, a time beyond time, a time of waiting, trusting and listening.

The Gathering

Step 7

A Time Beyond Time

The Heart of The Gathering

Steps 1 through 6 have prepared us for the heart of The Gathering, a "time" beyond time. This is when we can experience God or at least sow a seed that will bear fruit in the coming days.

The prayer and meditation practices of the religions and spiritual movements of humanity are many and varied, but most of them do two things: They help us focus our attention and clarify our motivation, and they lift us up in consciousness where we learn to wait. It is not important which of the prayer and meditation methods we use. What is crucial is that our purpose for the practice be conscious union and oneness with the One. This pure motivation helps us transcend the practice and learn to wait. We learn our prayer / meditation method, but above all, we learn to wait.

The time beyond time is the gift of Step 7, for it is when transformation takes place. Seeds are planted in these quiets moments that bear fruit not in our lives, but as our lives. Here are two images for prayer / meditation that lie at the heart of my interior life. Each stresses learning to wait.

The High Meadow

I am climbing a mountain and come to a beautiful, high meadow. Wild flowers are blooming and the long grasses of the field lie in the direction of the prevailing winds. I look down the slopes of the mountain into the valley and have a new perspective on the terrain below. There is a temptation to remain in this peaceful place, to think that I have arrived, but I am bound for the summit of the mountain.

I look for the trailhead of the path to the top of the mountain, but it is obscured by fog and mist. I cannot find my way, so I must wait. Wait for what or for whom? I wait for a woman to emerge from the mist to take me by the hand into the mystery of the mountain and onward to the summit. The woman's name is Grace.

The summit is an awareness of God's presence. Your prayer and meditation practice is the effort that brings you to The High Meadow. The truth is that there are many paths to The High Meadow. You can talk to God, sing, speak audible prayers or affirmations, and intone single sounds or mantras. You can read Scripture or give complete attention to the light of a candle. You can sit or wash the dishes with conscious attention. The list is nearly infinite, for there are countless practices that bring you to The High Meadow. I have even used the fragrance of essential oils to help me center my attention during times of inner reflection and contemplation.

The High Meadow is an elevated state of human consciousness. There is often peace and perhaps some spiritual insights here, for you have a new perspective on many things, but it is not the summit of the mountain. You cannot ascend the heights on your own or through your efforts. It is only through grace that you experience the summit.

The true work is waiting at The High Meadow. Waiting is the key to the time beyond time. Beyond time there is no thought, feeling or image. As the faculties of being, thinking, feeling and imagination slumber, a consciousness of pure silence is discovered.

* * * * * * *

Putting on Your Wings

There is a high bluff. Prevailing winds consistently cause an updraft from below that soars high
over the cliff. Birds sense the updraft. They flap their
wings to gain altitude, and when they feel the strong
thrust of the rising air current, they "put on their
wings." They stretch out their wings, and the rising
air currents lift them effortlessly as they spiral to a
greater height.

This flight is similar to many prayer and meditation methods. Our practice is the flapping of our
wings. It is the effort that we make to rise in consciousness. We are lifting ourselves, but the instant
we put on our wings, we cease our work and begin
to wait. Waiting for the unseen presence of the wind
to lift us is the same as waiting for Grace on the
mountain of God. Something beyond us, something
that transcends our humanity is required before we
are lifted to the height of God's presence.

Obviously, climbing to The High Meadow is
important, and it is also vital that the birds flap their
wings if they are to ride the ascending air currents,
but what is absolutely crucial is that we put on our
wings, that we wait at The High Meadow. If we can
do this and have our yearning be for God, we are
fulfilling the essence of Step 7. Our work can be as

simple as speaking or thinking the highest truth we know and waiting for Spirit to take us higher.

God's Prayer

For thousands of years, humanity has believed prayer is something we do, but this is not true. If prayer is an experience of God's presence and it comes through grace, prayer is what God does. We practice; God perfects. We wait, God lifts.

While we wait, we learn humility, compassion, nonresistance, patience, acceptance and self-love. These are the qualities we value most in other people and in the world. We may strive to live this way and express these qualities, but we fail. We fail because these qualities cannot live in the world until they live in us.

Waiting humbles us. We discover how powerless we are to make changes within ourselves. We try, expend effort, and strive with noble intentions, but we fail to realize that transformation is divine work. The waiting humbles us and opens us to powers and methods we do not understand. Eventually our efforts cease. This happens when divine efforts are best felt and experienced. We let go and "let God be God."[1]

As we wait, we are not passive. Our work is unconditional observation. We become sensitive to what is moving within us. Essentially we are answering the philosopher's maxim "Know thyself." We experience the feelings that move deep within us. We discover the thoughts that live in the depths of our soul. Memories emerge from a sheltered and often shameful or guilt-ridden past. The thoughts, feelings and memories are not always pleasant, but they do bring us the gift of the moment, and whenever we live in the moment we are truly alive.

As we wait, it is best if we are focused and centered. As stated before, there are myriad prayer practices, but it is good to have a safe home to return to. For instance, I often give my attention to one of the following ideas: *It Is, God Is, I Am.* Or on another occasion I inwardly declare, *God is enough.* The possibilities are infinite. I can even give attention to a physical object or an inner image.

I focus and then I wait. In most instances, the waiting is interrupted by thoughts, feelings or images. I do not condemn them or label them "good" or "bad." Each thought, feeling or image simply is. *It Is, God Is, I Am.* This is unconditional observation, and it teaches us compassion and acceptance of ourselves. We don't resist what is emerging from within;

we are watchers willing to discover what is moving within us beneath conscious thought and belief. In this way, we come to know ourselves and discover that before nonresistance can be effective in the world, it must be applied to that which moves in our souls.

We focus and wait and watch; the intrusion comes again. Without condemnation, without judgment, we observe and then declare our truth or engage in our prayer practice again, and then we wait only to be seized by the thought or feeling or image once more. Can you see how humbling this is?

Here is another example of waiting that most of us have experienced: the expected arrival of a friend at the airport. You will find waiting for a friend similar to waiting for the experience of the divine Friend. You stand at the end of the concourse from which your friend will emerge. While you wait, you see some people waiting as you are, and others lovingly greeting friends and family who have arrived before your friend. You observe the reunions and then return to the exit where your friend will emerge. Suddenly you see a police officer riding a Segway. You think, *That's a cool machine. I wish I had one. I wonder how much they cost. Is it hard to learn to ride one of those?*

* * * * * * *

You are distracted for a few moments from waiting for your friend, but now your eyes return to the exit and the people streaming from the concourse. You ask one of them what flight they were on. It's not the airline your friend took. You return to waiting and watching. Eventually your friend arrives. Your heart leaps for joy and you greet this dear one with open arms.

Haven't you experienced this form of waiting many times? You were patient, persistent and focused on the coming of your friend, but you were also distracted from your waiting. Your momentary lack of focus on the concourse exit did not mean you wanted to see your friend any less. Allowing yourself to be distracted did not mean you were a failure. The distractions were part of waiting. Waiting at the airport is a good example of the process we experience when we wait for God.

Eventually the Friend arrives, or more accurately, we discover a Presence that is always with us. We have an experience of the Presence. It may take weeks or even months, but persistence becomes a way of life. We discover a strength we never knew we possessed. We do not quit, for our quest is God. Most people report that the first experience of the Presence is a feeling of peace or comfort, but the truth

▪ ▪ ▪ ▪ ▪ ▪ ▪ ▪

is that Spirit can express Itself in a variety of ways. The outcome is that as we learn to wait, our consciousness is transformed. We become increasingly aware that God is real. We receive the gift of an awareness of Spirit. This is what lies beyond time. The gift of God perpetually offered to us is finally received. This consciousness becomes our life and is the glass through which we see ourselves, others and the world. What greater vision could there be? What greater gift could we receive? Above all, we learn to wait.

Taking the Step

If you are using the steps of The Gathering personally, you need only clarify that your purpose is to experience God's presence and then engage in your prayer practice or meditation method. After a time, cease the practice and wait without condemnation or judgment. Become the watcher and note what is moving within you. It is all self-knowledge. Wait, listen, trust, and when the mind wanders, gently bring it home again by using your practice or method once more ... and then wait again. Grace is coming. The unseen wind is rising.

If Step 7 is taken as a group, your leader probably determines the prayer practice or meditation method, but the true work remains the same—the waiting. Trust, listen and let God be God.

After a period of waiting, take Step 8 and allow it to bring you back into a consciousness of the beauty of the earth and the realm where there is space and time or, as we are discovering from our physicists, space-time.

Step 8

I Have Learned, in Whatever State I Am, to Be Content.
Knowing God Is Enough.

The Choice

Some stunning words of the apostle Paul gave birth to Step 8. Not the statements of Saul, the brash persecutor of the early Christians who was transformed on the road to Damascus, but the imprisoned Paul who wrote in a letter: "For I have learned, in whatever state I am, to be content" (Phil. 4:11 RSV). In his younger years, Paul was not content. The newly converted Christian could have never written about contentment, but as he matured and his spiritual life deepened, he found contentment and was able to let go of the need to bend life to his will.

* * * * * * * *

Like Paul, many of us have insisted that we know what is best for us. In fact, there is an approach to life that promises to provide us with tools to shape our lives according to our vision of the way it should be. We think about it, voice it, declare it, claim it and image it. We are told to be specific about our desires.

The person who adopts this way of life expects results. He knows exactly what he wants and goes after it. He may even achieve it, but there is a potential for anxiety, and contentment is not guaranteed. Achievements may accumulate in his world, but he does not possess himself. There is much that he claims to know, but he may not know his own soul. He knows exactly what he wants, but does not have a glimmer of understanding about who he is. He gets what he wants, but never discovers what God wants him to have. Would such a person ever say that *God is enough*? For this person, there is never enough because there is lack in the soul.

There is another way of life, more mysterious, but nevertheless filled with fulfillment and contentment. While many people ask for many things, people who enter into this mystery ask for only one thing—an awareness of God. They want to know that God is real; they want to know who they are.

· ■ ■ ■ ■ ■ ·

This is our choice. We can ask for many things, or we can yearn for a consciousness of the One. Our attention can be split and given to many things, or we can give attention to God. We can be specific about the worldly things we want, or specific about the one thing that can bring us contentment and help us transcend the world.

The Single Eye

Part of the mystery of the contented life is that while we initially do not know how an awareness of God will impact our life and prove relevant to daily living, there is an intuitive feeling that a treasure is being offered to us. Often we have tried to conceive our life and failed to find contentment, and so now we are willing to step into mystery and allow ourselves to be led down a path few have trod. Perhaps you are such a person. Have you worked and worked and found discontent to be your major accomplishment? Do you yearn for simplicity and believe that the essence of life transcends earthly matters? Have you come to value contentment and sensed that it can be found within you rather than in the world? Does the idea of an inner journey appeal to you?

* * * * * * *

If you resonate with any of these questions, you may soon discover a single door opening to a vast kingdom of joy and contentment. Enter through this door, and your need will be added unto you without you having to make it the object of your life's striving.

The door that stands before you is a consciousness of God. It requires a single eye to see it. It is interesting, if not puzzling, that when we yearn for one thing, an awareness of Spirit, everything is within our grasp. All we need for daily life is available, but we no longer make these needs the center of our lives. God is enough.

Giving ourselves to God, we let go of the world, and we no longer feel its heavy burden. We have God, and God is enough. This is Jesus' way of life. "Seek first the kingdom ... and all these things [what you will eat, drink, and wear] shall be added to you" (Mt. 6:33 NKJV). Even the ancients knew this secret to life, for it is written in Psalm 34:10 that "those who seek the Lord lack no good thing." This is not God giving you what you want; it is God appearing as your life. Is this enough for you or do you require more?

Life in the 21st century can be complex. It doesn't have to be, but often in the clamor for security we make it so. We fail to make the choices that can bring contentment because our "schedule" chooses what we do. Our basic choice is to make the schedule and follow it. I have certainly been guilty of this approach to life. In fact, I have struggled to find balance. The good news is that I always knew there could be balance between a spiritual life and the activities of being a husband, father and minister.

Long ago, I saw the promise in Jesus' call to seek first the kingdom of God. If I could only find that kingdom, all else would be added to me. I decided to put this verse of Scripture to the test. If it was true, I would give myself to living this truth and sharing this way of life with the world, and if it proved false, my search for a meaningful and productive life would continue, but in a different direction.

As you can tell, it passed my test, which was actually my life. You truly can give yourself to a spiritual way of life without having to give undue attention to the activities of the world. Of course, they require attention, but the underlying motivation can always be to seek to become aware of the Presence.

I have discovered that the promise is fulfilled, if I seek. There is little else I have to do initially. The seeking, the firm establishment of a desire to become aware of Spirit, sets the course, and Spirit shows the way. Action is often required, but it is deferred action. I act, but only when I feel a sense of direction.

If guidance is to be sensed, it is my responsibility to be sensitive to the movement of Spirit within me and to listen. The act of listening, stillness and silence become a part of the way I live my life.

Recently I decided to get up a littler earlier each morning so I can work out and still have nearly a half an hour to simply sit and be still. This is usually not a time of prayer and meditation as much as it is a time of receptivity. I am opening to the day and leaning inward to see what I might see and hear what I might hear.

As I meet with individuals or groups of people during the day, the sessions begin with five minutes of silence. And, of course, there is an evening time of prayer and meditation before retiring for the day and the ever-present attempt to practice the Presence of God, the union of daily life and the remembrance of spiritual events, truths and practices.

I have always loved the story in the third chapter of Daniel about Shadrach, Meshach and Abednego. It is truly a "God is enough" story. It is the time of the Babylonian captivity. Shadrach, Meshach and Abednego are in Babylon under the dominion of King Nebuchadnezzar II. The king has erected a

■ ■ ■ ■ ■ ■ ■ ■

golden stature of himself and requires that the people bow before it. Those who refuse to bow to the image die in a furnace of blazing fire. Our three young men believe in and give power to one God, and therefore they will not bow before the statue. Their act of defiance is brought to the attention of Nebuchadnezzar. The king is infuriated and has Shadrach, Meshach and Abednego brought before him.

There are powerful messages in this story, too many to probe in this chapter, but here is a message we must not miss. When threatened with death, the three captive Hebrews respond, "We have no need to present a defense to you in this matter. If our God whom we serve is able to deliver us from the furnace of blazing fire and out of your hand, O king, let him deliver us. But if not, be it known to you, O king, that we will not serve your gods and we will not worship the golden statue that you have set up" (Dan. 3:16-18). The king is filled with rage and orders the furnace made seven times hotter than before. It is so hot that the men stoking the fire perish from its heat. This is intimidation, but Shadrach, Meshach and Abednego stand fast.

They are cast into the fire, and King Nebuchadnezzar notices that there are now four figures in the fire and one "has the appearance of a

* * * * * * *

god." I believe that this story is the foundation for Jesus' statement, "For where two or three are gathered in my name, I am there among them" (Mt. 18:20). As you are now aware, this verse of Scripture is also at the heart of The Gathering.

Shadrach, Meshach and Abednego are released and they don't even smell of smoke. There are untouched by the situation. This story holds great promise for us and The Gathering. When God is enough, all else is given.

What You Can Know

Do you need to look around the bend? Do you need to know what the future holds? If you could predict the future, would you be secure and content? Are you insecure because you do not know what is going to happen? Is this the only way you can be content? Is this the only way you can face life? Can you live with the unknown? It is all around you, not a foe, but a friend whispering of the benefits of faith and bringing adventure and excitement to life.

Dear friend, you cannot know the future. The only thing you can know is God and this knowing is enough. Remember the creation story. Each day began with "Let there be." Letting seems to carry with it the insight that certain things are natural.

They come into being, if we let them. God let there be light, and it gave birth to the universe. Even as we emerged from the womb of creation, that part of God that is Mother cried out, "Let there be ... let us make man in our image."

Making things happen has been humanity's method of creation, and with every creation came tension, strain and anxiety. Those who adhere to God's method of creation, of letting, cry out, "I have learned, in whatever state I am, to be content." When we let go, something greater than ourselves can come into being, and with it comes contentment and joy.

We have a choice. We can hold on, or we can be held. When we hold on, we know exactly what we want, but we don't know who we are. We never find ourselves. Rather than enter into the mystery of creation, we remain a mystery to ourselves.

Those who know that God is enough are not only content, they are also nonresistant. Remember Jesus before Pilate? Pilate wielded the might of Rome. Jesus was an instrument of the power of God. Most people who think they possess power want to exercise it. Some who believed in Jesus expected him to wield the power of God and overthrow Rome, but those who know true power do not bring it to bear; they allow it to flow from within them. They may

■ ■ ■ ■ ■ ■ ■

bear injustice and do not resist the power of man. Why? Jesus, for instance, did not act because he knew Pilate had no real power. No cross could diminish Jesus' consciousness of his Father. No spear could pierce his love for humanity. Long before the crucifixion, divine love had pierced his heart, and what flowed forth was not blood but a life of service, humility, nonresistance, loving acceptance and contentment. It is the life that all are called to live.

Taking the Step

If you are using The Gathering for your personal prayer practice, you need only speak or think the words of Step 8: *I have learned, in whatever state I am, to be content. God is enough.*

If you are using The Gathering as a group prayer practice, the group leader asks the people present to affirm Step 8 out loud in unison. This step seals the time of reflection and is a benediction to the spiritual journey that is The Gathering. Only the three reminders remain. The section of the book entitled "How to Form and Conduct a Gathering" provides more details of how Step 8 concludes the "Time Beyond Time."

The Gathering

Step 9

The Three Reminders

The Gathering concludes with three reminders. After the time of reflection and acknowledging that God is enough, gently return to an awareness of your surroundings. If you have shared the steps as a group, the leader can share with the members of The Gathering the three reminders. The first reminder: *There is to be no discussion of what happened in our interior world during the time of prayer and meditation.*

As our prayer/meditation life deepens, there may be times when voices are heard, images seen, or physical sensations felt. These phenomena and others are called consolations by mystics. It is important that we give little attention to such things, for they can divert our focus from our quest of experiencing the presence and power that God is. Rather than seeking the kingdom, we seek the consolations.

Anyone who embarks upon the inner journey will face this temptation. In prayer and meditation groups, there is a tendency for people to want to share the consolations. They are erroneously viewed as evidence of spirituality. As we shall see in the second reminder, there is also a tendency, when individuals in a group share their consolations, for some of the people to think they have failed because they are not having similar experiences. Regrettably, they may try "keeping up with the Joneses."

In Chapter 10 of the Revelation, John is asked to eat a small scroll. This scroll is symbolic of a body of teachings or experiences. He eats the scroll and is told it will taste sweet in his mouth, but bitter in his stomach.

This revelation brings to light an important aspect of the spiritual journey. There are teachings or experiences that are sweet in our mouths. They entice us and tantalize us, but they do not nourish us. They are bitter in the stomach.

The consolations may excite us, but they are not what we seek. They provide no true sustenance, so they should be put aside as we again seek in the silence an experience of our God. Psychic phenomena are an example of the scroll that is sweet in the mouth and bitter in the stomach.

■ ■ ■ ■ ■ ■ ■ ■

If we choose to "eat this scroll," we delay our spiritual journey because we are sidetracked into thinking such teachings or phenomena are evidence of spiritual growth. The lower self, the ego, loves to have us think we are on the path when we have strayed from our course and are no longer seeking the kingdom. This is one of the reasons the first reminder is important. There is another.

Many years ago, my wife Nancy and I attended a spiritual retreat in which there was an Emmaus Walk. The foundation of this walk is found in Luke 24. Two men were on their way to Emmaus, a village seven miles from Jerusalem. As they walked, they talked about the events surrounding Jesus' crucifixion, and he joined them, but they did not recognize him. After sharing a meal with Jesus, their eyes were opened, and they recognized him.

During an Emmaus Walk, groups of two people are asked, through a series of questions, to talk about spiritual things. The idea is that when this is done, the Christ will join the two individuals. In other words, the spirit of God is released from each of the people, and their eyes are opened.

While Nancy was on her walk, she and her partner saw a deer. This was the first time Nancy had ever seen a deer in the wild. It was a spiritually

▪ ▪ ▪ ▪ ▪ ▪ ▪

enlivening experience for her. Later that morning during another outside spiritual activity, Nancy rushed back to the previous location to repeat the experience of seeing the deer, but there was no deer to see. She was disappointed, but then realized that she was trying to duplicate an event that had awakened her spiritually.

As soon as she let go of the need to repeat the previous day's experience, the deer appeared again. Lesson learned. This is one of the main points of the first reminder. We are not to try to duplicate spiritual experiences. We give thanks for them and let them go.

The second reminder: *We are not to grade ourselves on how well we are doing in our prayer life. "All is well" is a phrase we like to use.*

The Gathering is not a means to an end. We are not trying to find an answer to life's problems, although solutions and insights may come to us; however, we are seeking to firmly establish a way of life through the steps of The Gathering.

Consider this example. One person prays and meditates and experiences a sense of oneness with the One. There is peace and a feeling of connectedness to the whole. Another person's meditative experience is markedly different. His mind wanders, and he never finds peace. He is anxious and does not enter a state of consciousness of contentment or unity with his world. The next day both individuals continue to pray and meditate. The one who experienced consolations is eager to pray and meditate again. Why? It may be to duplicate the previous experience. (Obviously this is not always the case when a person has a powerful experience with the Presence, but most people who are developing a meditative life face this challenge.) The person whose mind wandered is again seeking the kingdom. Which of the two individuals is firmly upon the path?

It is the person who could not find his peace the previous evening. The reason there is progress is that this person is exhibiting persistence and spiritual strength. He remains true to the purpose of knowing God. The other individual has lost his way. He no longer seeks the kingdom; he wants the gifts of Spirit rather than Spirit Itself. Remember, this is a challenge we all will face.

Nearly everyone who has a beautiful experience during a Gathering or a personal time of reflection will return to pray and meditate the next day. In many instances, the person seeks a repeat performance from the previous time of contemplation. In that moment, the seeker is no longer seeking God. This

* * * * * * *

path is not one of seeking consolations. We are not yearning to repeat previous experiences, to eat from day-old bread. Our spirituality is daily bread, baked fresh with the rising of the sun. This is one of the messages of the first reminder.

The individual who seemed to "fail," but who is once more committing to the inner journey, is developing spiritual strength that will serve him or her well in the days to come.

It is not important how well we think we are doing. There is no grade for participation in a Gathering or deepening our prayer life. Skills are being developed, but our real commitment is to a way of life. *All is well* is a helpful phrase to hold in mind.

The third reminder: *What is important is that we have gathered in God's name, and we will gather again.* In this reminder, can you hear the call to persistence? Can you sense the spiritual strength rising up in you?

We persist in gathering in God's name. During biblical times, a person's name often revealed something about his or her nature. Remember Jacob whose name means "supplanter"? Through deception he stole his father Isaac's blessing. He took advantage of his hungry brother to acquire Esau's birthright as the future patriarch of the family. There

* * * * * * * *

was a time in his life when he embodied the meaning of his name. However, after a spiritual experience at Jabbok Ford that changed him, his name was changed to Israel, which means "prince of God."

When we gather in God's name, we gather in God's nature. We come together as a group of seekers or as an individual yearning for conscious oneness with our Creator. We revel in God's nature knowing it is our own. In truth, God's nature is at the foundation of the steps of The Gathering.

Some steps reveal God's willingness to give and express Itself as our very being. Love is at the foundation of steps that ask us to forgive ourselves and others. We are even asked to accept ourselves as we are. Another step stresses the importance of waiting and letting God be God. One teaches us of the nature of awareness and how it is God's avenue into our lives and the world. And finally, Step 9 calls us to gather again and again and again.

Taking the Step

If you are using The Gathering for your personal prayer practice, there is no need to speak the reminders verbally, but please read them and call to mind why they are important to your prayer life.

If you are using The Gathering as a group prayer practice, the group leader simply reminds the members of the group about the three reminders. It is important that each person understand why the three reminders are a part of The Gathering.

A 40-Day Guide to
The Gathering

Now you know the promise of a Gathering. A power greater than self is available to you. Joined with others or alone in your home, you can experience the presence of God. The nine steps of a Gathering take you on a spiritual journey into your own being and ask that you view the world in a new way. In this practice, you are never alone, for there are others who are gathering just as you are and who now view life from a similar vantage point. The Gathering has helped you discover what has always been present. It has helped to open your eyes and to expand your awareness.

The previous chapters have explained the foundation ideas of each of the nine steps. You know the spiritual principles upon which The Gathering was built. Now it is time to build a bridge that extends from what you have read to the life you live. As you cross this bridge, you will move from concept to the events of your exterior and interior life.

Even if you have already begun to utilize the steps of The Gathering, I recommend you complete the 40-day guide, for as you explore your life in relationship

. . . .

to each of the steps, new insights will come that will make The Gathering an even better friend than it is now.

You might wonder why 40 days. The answer is that it occurs symbolically in the Bible. It rained for 40 days and 40 nights and floodwaters engulfed the earth. The Hebrews wandered 40 years in the wilderness before entering the Promised Land. Jesus prepared for his temptations by fasting for 40 days. We have a number here that symbolizes the length of time required to complete a task. However, it may take you more than 40 literal days to complete the Guide. It is designed so you can move from one day to another, but you may want to linger with the ideas and practices of a particular day.

The 40-Day Guide summarizes the ideas found in the book, but it also asks you to walk the bridge and venture not only deeper into the ideas in *The Gathering*, but also to move deeper into your life. The practices of the Guide may help you remember long forgotten memories or enable you to see a past hurt or your previous behavior from a different perspective. You cannot change what has happened, but you can certainly see it through new eyes. Your new vision will enable you to relate the steps of The Gathering to your life.

You are encouraged to write in the guide portion of the book so you will have a record of your thoughts, feelings and perceptions at this time in your life. Years later you may return to these pages and receive additional insight into the person you have become.

Enjoy the experience of the 40-Day Guide, and remember that you are not alone. I have crossed this bridge and so have others who found The Gathering to be a spiritual practice that reveals a God who is both present and a practical help in daily living.

But I have needs!

We have cried out, "We have needs. We want them resolved. We have the need to be healed, prospered, loved, and the need to know what to do." The list of needs seems endless. Often we have found a way to fulfill our needs. It bolstered our confidence, so when another need surfaced, we moved forward with the conviction that we could solve this problem too; however, there were also times when we felt helpless. The need seemed too great, so we presented it to God. We thought, *Perhaps God could take care of the need.* Since that time we have learned another way, but we must admit this was our beginning.

What needs have you resolved in your life seemingly through your own efforts?

What needs have you presented to God and hoped God would resolve? Were the needs met to your satisfaction?

Is there a need in your life today? If so, what is it? Are you solving it yourself or have you presented it to God?

DAY 1

A need is not an avenue of God's expression.

The realization that a need is not an avenue through which Spirit can do Its work is one of the greatest insights we can receive. I cannot count the many angry words I have shouted or how many times I have shaken my fist to the heavens because I thought God had forsaken me or ignored my needs.

Often we have a need we know we cannot solve, so we ask God to help. Surely Spirit would act on our behalf. This is what we believe, but often we find that the need remains. God did not answer our plea. At that time, we did not know that a need is not an avenue of God's expression, so we chose to believe God either could not or would not assist us. There were times when we were angry with God, times when we wondered if our past negative behavior and unresolved guilt were the reasons the need remained.

Here are some questions to help you examine your own feelings of need.

Have you ever been angry with God because you believed God would not help you? What was the need? How long did the feeling linger?

If you have a current need, are you willing to declare, *This need is not an avenue through which God can act? Something else is required.* If so, please write the affirmation in the space provided.

DAY 2

. . . .

Needs turn me to God.

Today we hear the whispered message of every need we have ever experienced. *Don't present me to God; present yourself to God. Don't focus on me; focus on God.*

Dear friend, each need is saying, "Don't look at me. Gently put me aside and then look to God." If you do this, the purpose of every need is fulfilled, and you will be closer not only to a potential resolution of your challenge, but also closer to God.

Using the italicized statements above as a foundation, write a meditation that you can use in the days to come when a need is demanding your attention and asking you to present it to God. Please conclude your written meditation with the following idea. *Now I remember; the role of a need is to turn me to God.*

DAY 3

This practice will help you understand the role of needs in your life. They turn us to God. Once this is accomplished, you can release the need.

DAY 3

Today is a day of remembering.

Today we remember what God is doing. God is being … being the Source, being Love, being Wisdom, being Strength, being Life, being Peace. Having gently put aside our need and turned to God, we no longer ask God to act on our behalf. God is doing all God can do, and it is enough. We must become aware of what God is doing. When we do, we become a wick in God's candle, and God's light can shine. Spirit has an avenue through which to express as the Source, Love and Wisdom.

When you consider your challenge, what remembrance of what God is doing will help you through your challenge? For instance, if you have a prosperity challenge, knowing God to be your Source can bring you security and well-being. If you have a healing need, knowing God to be Life can bring you an awareness of wholeness and heal your physical and mental disease.

DAY 4

Why do you think remembering what God is doing rather than asking God to act on your behalf is a more effective spiritual practice?

DAY 4

An awareness of the presence of God is an avenue through which Spirit can do Its work.

It was astonishing to learn that a need is not an avenue through which Spirit can do Its work. This realization may shock us and, for a time, we feel helpless and without hope, but then we make a discovery. Whenever we become aware of the presence of God, a doorway forms through which God's power can pour. This brings us hope and gives us direction for our spiritual lives. We can actually experience God's presence and power.

Here is the image that was shared in Chapter 1. A candle may potentially provide hours of light and warmth, but a wick is required. Unless there is a wick, the light and warmth remain locked within the wax. Just as a candle needs a wick, so Spirit needs someone to become aware of It. Whenever this occurs, a wick is provided, and God's wisdom and love radiate through that person into his or her life and into the world.

DAY 5

Today, please hold a simple thought in mind: *I am a wick in God's candle.* Record your experience with this idea in the space below.

DAY 5

Today I ponder three statements of truth.

This is a day of reflection and contemplation. From the time you rise in the morning until noon, please hold in mind the following idea: *God knows what I need before I ask.*

Record any insights that come to you about that idea in the space below.

DAY 6

From noon until 6 p.m., please hold in mind the following idea: *There are no needs in God.*
Record any insights that come to you in the space below.

From 6 p.m. until you go to bed, please ponder the following idea: *Needs turn me to God.*
Record any insights that come to you in the space below.

DAY 6

I have discovered the real issue.

We must admit that for many years our personal goal has been to be rid of the pain, limitation and anguish we have felt. We have made one attempt after another to be free of these concerns and their associated problems. At times, our diligent efforts seemed to succeed, only to find that after a time the problems reappeared. On a good day, we would rededicate ourselves to overcoming these challenges; on a bad day, we slipped momentarily into hopelessness and began to feel desperate.

But then we discovered the real issue. Were we meant to perpetually strive to rid ourselves of our problems, or was our true quest to express our spiritual nature? If we discovered our true self, would the discovery naturally dissipate the seeming power of our challenges? This is a question worthy of being answered, but we knew it would take us on a new journey, a journey that could actually bring us peace and joy. This is the path we now take.

The idea in today's lesson is to become a constant companion. You are to cease your efforts to change conditions and instead give yourself to the discovery of your true nature. Please hold in mind the following idea: *I give myself to the real issue—discovering and expressing my spiritual nature.*

DAY 7

Whenever you are tempted to solve a problem, remember the real issue and write in the space below, *I give myself to the real issue—discovering and expressing my spiritual nature.*

DAY 7

Acceptance is a step I take so I can express my spiritual nature.

It seems irrational that there is power in acceptance. We have thought acceptance was capitulation and weakness. Acceptance would not be a step forward, but a step backwards. We don't want to live with limitation, pain or anguish. Surely, if we accept the negative conditions of our lives, unhappiness will follow us all the days of our lives.

These are the thoughts of the typical person. We believe we must eliminate the problem or run far away from it so it cannot touch us, but the manifestation of consciousness is a problem. Acceptance is not surrender; it is nonresistance and the acknowledgment of the beginning of a divine process.

There are two reasons for acceptance. When we are accepting, resistance ceases, and we can express our divinity. Let today be a day of trust. Humanity has tried to eradicate its problems for millennia with little success. Now is the time to take another approach. Our purpose is not to eliminate problems; it is to discover and express our true nature.

DAY 8

In the space provided below, please list three challenges of your life, past or current, and the methods you used to try to solve them.

After completing the exercise, write: *I take the next step. I cease trying to change the conditions of my life and open myself to experience my true nature.*

DAY 8

Acceptance is nonresistance in action.

Acceptance does not seem like action. Acceptance appears passive, but it is a great force for good. Many spiritual giants have asked us to "resist not." We are to cease our efforts to solve our problems because our actions often grow out of anger, frustration, fear or doubt. Little is achieved when we act from such feelings and our primary purpose is solving the problem.

War is a problem we have not solved, and yet peace has been the hope of sane people in every age. We long for a world without disease, prejudice and poverty, but these three issues have challenged every generation. Surely we are not supposed to accept such conditions.

Remember, acceptance does not mean a challenge cannot be met. It means a different method is to be discovered and put to use. Acceptance causes our previous, well-intentioned efforts to stop so that a new consciousness can unfold, one that allows us to see a way that can actually succeed.

Are you willing to cease your previous efforts at trying to solve a problem in your life? Notice that you are not asked to cease your efforts at solving other problems; however, it is suggested that you give acceptance a chance before you continue as you have before. Acceptance is not passive. It is a special kind of nonresistance. It is a pause that slows

■ ■ ■ ■ ■ ■ ■

unproductive momentum. It is the first step in a new way of resolving your challenges.

In the space provided below, answer the question *Are you willing to cease your previous efforts at trying to solve a problem in your life?* **I hope you will write one simple word—Yes!**

DAY 9

I accept ...

Today's work is simple. It is to make a list of things in our lives we need to accept. Make a list of at least 10 things. If you are unable to assemble 10 items, please bookmark this page and return to it when another item makes itself known to you. This will not take long because daily life tends to present us with opportunities to resist, to effect an outer change without the pursuit and discovery of our true selves.

Here are a few possibilities to get you started.

I accept the weather as it is.

I accept my body as it is.

I accept my child as she or he is.

I accept my mother-in-law as she is.

I accept my father-in-law as he is.

I accept myself as I am.

I accept my memories, my feelings and my thoughts as they are.

With this exercise, you are beginning a new way of life. Can you feel it? Write your list in the space below.

DAY 10

. . . .

I accept myself the way I am.

Today is an important day, for we begin the work of accepting ourselves the way we are. We do not resist our thoughts, feelings or memories. They are what they are. We do not shy away from them. We will be fully alive and therefore fully human.

This takes courage. Most of us try to hide the parts of ourselves we find unacceptable. We create layers of disguise. The problem is not that we hide our unacceptable parts, but that our hidden humanity covers our spiritual nature. We are unaware of our true self, and it is only through this self that the challenges of life are met. To accept ourselves is to love ourselves. This enables us to be fully alive and to experience life to the fullest.

Today's exercise will most likely challenge you, but it makes Step 2 personal. It will be more than a step; it will be the beginning of a new way of life.

Indicate a condition in your life you find unacceptable and then write below it *I accept this condition just the way it is.*

Indicate a feeling in your life you find unacceptable and then write below it *I accept this feeling just the way it is.*

Indicate a thought or belief in your life you find unacceptable and then write below it *I accept this thought/belief just the way it is.*

Indicate a memory in your life you find unacceptable and then write below it *I accept this memory just the way it is.*

Indicate a person in your life you find unacceptable and then write below the name *I accept this person just the way s/he is.*

▪ ▪ ▪ ▪ ▪ ▪ ▪

I am not alone.
My dear Friend is at my side and closer than hands and feet.

This is the day you are called to put to the test the "Friend at My Side" prayer practice revealed in Step 2. This will enable you to genuinely accept a feeling or memory that has troubled you, perhaps for years. At least, it will be a beginning. Please know that you may need to repeat the prayer practice until a breakthrough is complete. Turn to Step 2 and read the section entitled "Love Yourself" (16-20) that outlines the prayer practice.

Next determine a time when you can test the "Friend at My Side" prayer practice. It may be hours from now. This is acceptable because it will build anticipation as you give yourself to God and the healing of the past and the associated emotions.

Once you determine when you can share some time with your "Friend," consider what feeling or memory you currently find unacceptable and with which you want to make peace. All that remains is for you to put the prayer practice to the test.

In the space provided, indicate the feeling or memory and then describe the experience of your "Friend at My Side" meditation.

DAY 12

Thank you for being here.
Thank you for standing and speaking.

This is the day you are called to put to the test another prayer practice found in Step 2—"The Banquet." This practice will enable you to continue to accept yourself the way you are. Please know that you may need to repeat the prayer practice until the breakthrough occurs. Turn to Step 2 and read the section entitled "The Banquet" that outlines the prayer practice.

Next determine a time when you can test the Banquet prayer practice. It may be hours from now. This is acceptable because it will build anticipation as you give yourself to God and the healing of the past and the associated emotions.

Once you determine when you can invite your friends and conduct the Banquet, consider what feeling or memory you currently find unacceptable and with which you want to make peace. All that remains is for you to put the prayer practice to the test.

DAY 13

* * * * * * *

In the space provided, indicate the feeling or memory and then describe the experience of your Banquet meditation.

DAY 13

Step by step, God is becoming more real to me.

By now you know that this 40-Day Guide is progressively taking you through the ideas in *The Gathering* and asking you to make them live by personalizing the various concepts and ideas. This inner journey will continue, but let us pause for a day to insure that you are also using the steps as a foundation for your daily prayer practice. Not everyone has a group of like-minded friends with which to share The Gathering. And besides, it is an outstanding approach to spirituality that can be put to the test in your home.

I want to support you as you dedicate yourself to The Gathering. As you encounter challenges with a particular step, please contact me through my Inner Journey website (*www.innerjourney.org*) and outline the difficulty you are having. I will respond as soon as I can with what I hope will be helpful insights. At the least, you will know you are not alone and that someone cares about you and your relationship with a power greater than self.

DAY 14

* ▪ ▪ ▪ ▪ ▪ ▪ ▫

In the space below, record any difficulties you are having as you use the steps of The Gathering and then share them with me via the website.

DAY 14

I acknowledge that there are parts of me that are barriers to an experience of God's presence.

This could be a challenging assignment. It requires great personal integrity. It is evident that our spiritual journey has reached a point where our quest is not of the world; we want to know and experience the presence and power of God. Spirit is not in hiding. God has erected no barriers to the oneness we seek. Barriers are present, and we are their builders.

This is the beginning—acknowledging that there are barriers and that they are our creation. Next we want to know what stands between us and a relationship with our God so they can be released.

Form in your mind's eye a wall or a barrier, and see yourself standing before it. Examine it closely because it is of your construction. It is formed from the content of your own consciousness. Its appearance, the materials out of which it is made, its height, length and depth are a message to you. It is possible the barrier may even speak to you.

DAY 15

As you explore the barrier, determine if there is a
way beyond the wall or barrier. Is it possible for
the barrier to become a bridge allowing you to
move forward in your life?

You have explored the wall with your eyes; now
touch it. What is its texture? Does the texture provide any hints to the barriers you have erected
between you and your God?

Now close your eyes and listen. Let the barrier
speak to you. What does it say?

Write any insights that come to you as you explore
the barrier. They may be useful in the days to
come.

DAY 15

Willingness is my beginning.

It is one thing to become acquainted with the barriers we have erected between us and a consciousness of the Presence; it is quite another thing to release them and let them go. Some barriers have become friends, for they have been with us a long time. We don't know how to live without them. To release them would be to embark upon a new life, a life unknown to us, so we hold on instead of allowing ourselves to be held.

When this occurs, our next step is simply to state our willingness to release and let go. We may not be able to actually take the step of releasing the barriers, but we are willing. For today, willingness is enough.

In the space below, write a statement of your willingness to let go of any part of your human self that is a barrier to God.

DAY 16

I now release that which stands between me and my God.

If we hold on to something, it must be because we believe it serves us in some way. However, those things that stand between our God and us do not serve the truth of our being; they serve the lower self. In fact, the lower self, the one we have created, needs to be served. It cannot stand on its own. We now withdraw our support from this false self.

In preparing to actually release the barriers we have erected between us and God, we construct a symbol in the mind that depicts this barrier. (Pause and let an image fill your mind.) Please know it will be consumed in the fire of God's presence.

It is now given to Spirit, and because it is not like God, it is no more. Form an image in your mind of the divine fire. It will not harm you, for you were forged in this fire. It gave you life. Now complete this process, and place the symbol in the fire and do not take your eyes away from it until the symbol is no more. All that remains is God.

DAY 17

Do you feel less burdened because you performed this mental imagery practice? What feeling do you have? Record your experience in the space below.

DAY 17

Letting go is my way of life.

The human self that we have created is made up of layer upon layer of false perceptions, attitudes and beliefs. This is why letting go and the practice of release are destined to become a way of life. In truth, the spiritual life is one of subtraction rather than addition. Nothing needs to be added to us, for we were created by the One who knows only perfection.

The good news is that The Gathering is a prayer and meditation practice that can be put to the test each day of our lives. Whenever we take Step 3, we are reminded that God is with us, but that we have erected barriers to our awareness of Spirit.

DAY 18

Dear friend, are you willing to establish letting go as a way of life? How will you bring to mind the need for releasing the barriers created by the human self?

DAY 18

I am willing to forgive others.

We begin with willingness once again. However much we may want to forgive and know it is vital for our spiritual growth and well-being, we may not be able to actually forgive because we feel justified in our anger and resentment. Nevertheless, we can begin this important part of our transformation with a willing heart.

Please know that unforgiveness is probably the most prevalent barrier to an experience of the presence of God. If suddenly everyone on earth was able to forgive, love would flow from our hearts and wars would end. We would no longer be blinded by our own perspectives, beliefs and viewpoints.

This is the promise of forgiveness. Today's statement brings a question to mind: If all the members of the human race declared their willingness to forgive, would anything constructive happen? We can surmise that global forgiveness would transform the world. What would global willingness do?

We may not be able to answer the question about willingness for the whole human race, but we can answer it for ourselves. As you work with today's idea, determine when you are truly willing to forgive. Does this make a difference in your life? Do you feel different? Can you sense a shift in yourself or a change of attitude?

■ ■ ■ ■ ■ ■ ■

If you do feel different and sense a constructive change in yourself, you will know without a doubt that willingness is an important step to take. In fact, just about any difficult task that is before us can begin with willingness. Once willingness is established, transformation has begun. It is such a humble, simple beginning that many people miss it. Not you. You know its power.

DAY 19

In the space below, write about your experience of willingness. Also, indicate what other parts of your life could benefit from your willingness?

Without forgiveness, I cannot feel the love of God.

In Step 4, it is written, "No one has a healthy, loving relationship with God who is in conflict with his fellow human beings, and it is only through a divine partnership with God that the power of the One flows in Its fullness into our lives." Can you see the implications of this statement? God is Love, and since we are made in God's image and likeness, loving must be the most natural thing for us to do. However, through our lack of forgiveness, we hide our true selves under the cover of anger and resentment. Obviously there are personal implications and ramifications to our lack of forgiveness, but the effect is also global.

Humanity has problems that cannot be solved by logic and human efforts. Spiritual awakening is demanded. The divine partnership is required, but it is not possible when we are at war with one another. Could it be that our inability to create a peaceful world is because of our lack of willingness to forgive one another our perceived wrongs? Global peace rises out of a collective willingness to forgiveness. And, of course, it begins with one person. That person could be you.

You can work with today's statement and feel the weight of your lack of willingness to forgive, but take it a step farther. Become the spokesperson for the human family. Say to the citizens of the world, "Without forgiveness, we cannot feel the love of God." Without an experience of God's presence, there can be no peace. This is why war persists. It has no human answer. The solution is divine, and it begins with forgiveness.

DAY 20

Then ask the human family, "Will there be peace?" How do they answer? Is there anyone who is a holdout? This one refuses to forgive; so great is his or her hurt. What will you do? Are you helpless? Are we helpless?

Today I forgive.

Today's work is simple, and it begins a most difficult part of our spiritual journey—forgiveness. In Step 4, there is a three-step forgiveness process. I trust that you have begun this work where necessary. The three steps are taken over a period of two months to allow for a consciousness of love to be born in you.

You may have a number of people currently in your life or from your past you want to forgive. You may wonder if it is necessary to take all three steps with each person. Good question.

It is necessary to forgive each one, for even the feelings you hold toward one person is enough to stand between you and an ever deepening experience of divine love; however, I do not think it is necessary to enter into the process with every person.

Here is my prediction. The purpose of the three-step forgiveness process is not simply to forgive someone; it is to establish in you a consciousness of love. Once this state of mind and heart lives in you, it will spread throughout your being and into all relationships. In ways I don't fully understand, I believe it will even touch your past relationships.

DAY 21

In the space provided, describe how the process outlined above can touch the past. After you have contemplated your answer, look at my answer below.

DAY 21

Feelings and memories do not live in the past but in your current moment; therefore, they impact you today. Do the work today, and you will find the "past" is healed.

■ ■ ■ ■ ■ ■ ■ ■

I no longer echo the negative, destructive things that people have said about me.

In the Step 5 section entitled "The Echo," I wrote about an event all of us have experienced. Someone says something about us that is hurtful and untrue. Because it is not true, we should simply ignore the statement, but often we echo it. The actual words do little damage. In fact, words cannot actually affect us. They are just words. However, the damage occurs when we doubt ourselves and begin to take up the chant and echo the words.

For instance, a person may say we are stupid. They may declare it with emotional power that impacts us. And then we do the unthinkable: we echo what has been said. We think about ourselves as stupid. We may never verbalize what we heard, but the idea has taken up residency in our mind.

As we expand our forgiveness work to include ourselves, we begin by probing our past and the lies we have echoed.

List on the next page at least five lies that you have heard spoken about you (perhaps long ago) that you are echoing in the silent recesses of your mind. Write the lie and follow it with the truth. After the completion of today's exercise, write an

DAY 22

additional statement that will become a pledge that you will never knowingly echo a lie about yourself ever again.

Lie:
Truth:

Lie:
Truth:

Lie:
Truth:

Lie:
Truth:

Lie:
Truth:

The Pledge

DAY 22

This is good work that you are doing today. It is preparing the way for the realization that you are precious to God.

· ■ ■ ■ ■ ■ ■ ■

There is nothing I have ever thought, said or done that can change what God has made.

As human beings we are powerful. There are many things we can do, but we have not been granted the power to change what God has made, and God's supreme creation, dear friend, is you.

We tend to think that what others say about us or do to us can defile us. How often has an abused child grown up to believe that there is something gravely wrong with him because of what was done to him long ago? The truth is that the adult is just as pure and beautiful and precious to God today as he was on the day of his creation.

Our thinking can certainly impact who we think we are and alter our view of ourselves and the world, but thoughts are not so powerful that they can alter what God has made. Dear friend, it is time to ask yourself, *What is the greatest power in my life?* Is it what has happened to you, what you have done, what you believe about yourself or what others believe about you?

Here's a thought. What if the greatest power was not of this world, but was the way in which you are actually made? If you knew yourself to be God's creation and untouched by the world, how would this change your life?

DAY 23

Write your answer below.

DAY 23

The mark of Cain is upon me.

Please reread the section "The Mark of Cain" in Step 5.

What does the mark of Cain say about you? What does it declare to the world? Write your answer below, and then write four additional interpretations of the mark of Cain that express the same sentiment expressed in Step 5.

DAY 24

If the mark of Cain was a tattoo, what would it look like? Where would the mark be on your body? Remember, it must be where all can see. When I consider such things, I wonder if there could be a look on a person's face that reveals that he or she is precious to God. What do you think?

DAY 24

Today I listen intently to my inner voices, so I can determine "who's on the phone."

Once we begin to explore our inner world, we "hear voices." Usually they take the form of thoughts. Thoughts move within us. Some support the spiritual journey. Some do not.

We know the power of acceptance, and therefore we do not ignore, resist or attempt to push aside the thoughts that live within us. We listen to them so we can determine who is on the phone.

There are thoughts that are the voice of God in us. The experience of hearing the Spirit of Truth in us can take many forms, but essentially the message is *You are precious to Me. You are My beloved.* Any messages you hear that do not support such ideas are not the voice of God; they are your ego or pygmy self telling its lies.

This insight is a powerful one, for it enables us to immediately determine who is on the phone. However, even the lies told by the ego can be helpful. The lies are simply information that reveals to us the attitudes or beliefs that live in us. Being able to identify them is an important part of the process of rendering them powerless.

What are the prevalent lies told to you by your ego? Remember, if the thoughts are not in some-way aligned to the statements on the previous page, they are lies.

DAY 25

There is nothing I can say or do that can change God's creation.

Many of us carry the burdensome belief that we are broken in some way. There may be people who affirm this is true, and there may be appearances that seem to proclaim our brokenness, but it is not true. Just how powerful are we? Are we so powerful that we can change what God has made?

Remember, Spirit has made us in Its image and likeness. The great news, in fact, the greatest news in our lives, is that no matter what has happened to us, we are as God created us. Once we begin to entertain such an idea, we can begin to forgive ourselves. All the things we have done, said, left undone and not said, have not changed the essence of us, what God has made.

There is a part of us that is just as pure now as we were on the day of our creation. This persistent truth calls us to forgive ourselves.

DAY 26

In the space below, write the following statement: *I am not broken; I am as God created me.* Pause for 30 seconds and write the first thing that comes to your mind. Then write the statement again and listen once more with a willingness to record whatever comes to you. Do this three times.

DAY 26

In the light of God,
there is no darkness.

We know that unforgiveness is a barrier to an experience of God's presence. We can hold ill feelings toward other people or ourselves. Since the focus in Step 5 is self-forgiveness, there are several practices in the chapter that can help with the important work of forgiving ourselves and living without guilt.

Have you ever felt that there was a darkness in you that needed to be healed? Perhaps Jesus was speaking of this when he said, "If your eye [where you place your focus] is unhealthy, your whole body will be full of darkness. If then the light that is in you is darkness, how great is the darkness!" (Mt. 6:23).

Here is another spiritual practice that came to me while contemplating this verse of Scripture. I hope it will be helpful to you.

Consider this strange image in which you are holding a candle that does not radiate light; it radiates darkness. Wherever you go shadows are cast. The darkness emanates from the guilt and self-loathing that is housed within.

Hold the candle, let it radiate its darkness, but go in search of the light of God. Walk carefully and eventually you will see a light in the distance. Move slowly toward it. It is calling you with Its beauty. Draw near to the light and hold out the candle. Notice that the darkness cannot penetrate or envelop the light of God, for the darkness is a no thing.

Stand in the light as the candle that was radiating darkness now ignites and radiates the divine light. The light of God did not resist the darkness or curse the guilt and self-loathing; it simply shone, and darkness was no more. You are healed. You no longer radiate darkness, for you are now a bearer of the light.

DAY 27

In the space below, indicate the first things you will do as a bearer of the light. I suggest that you begin with thanksgiving and then add three more actions that radiate God's light into the world.

. . . .

There is only one answer.

As human beings, we experience many problems or challenges. Could it be that there is only one answer? This seems impossible. The problems are too many and too diverse; however, what joy there would be if all challenges had a single answer.

Let us proceed with the possibility of only one answer. What would it be? Wouldn't the discovery of this answer be the greatest breakthrough of our century? Perhaps it would rank as one of the top discoveries of the human family.

For many years, I have been living my life from the assumption that there is only one answer—a consciousness of God. In fact, our inability to be aware of the Presence in which we live and move and have our being tends to perpetuate our difficulties.

As we become conscious of God, an avenue is created through which wisdom, strength, supply, love and power can flow and express. All that is needed for joyous, meaningful life is available to us. It is closer than hands and feet and breathing, but we must become aware of it. A consciousness of God allows us to see, to hear, to know and to be what we are.

Bookmark this page, for you will want to return to this exercise again and again. When you face your next challenge, resist the tendency to want to fix the

DAY 28

problem or to find a solution in the world. A solution will come, but it is not your first quest. Your initial step is to turn to God. We will not ask God to act or to tell us what to do. Instead we simply ask to become conscious of the presence and power God is. This is enough, for consciousness provides an avenue through which we discover what is needed and what we are to do.

In the space below, write the steps you will take so you can face your challenge and move beyond it.

Step 1:

Step 2:

Step 3:

Step 4:

What action did you take in the world that enabled you to put the challenge behind you?

DAY 28

* * * * * * *

Life is a consciousness of God.

The more we work with the idea that there is a single answer to the many and varied challenges of life, the better able we are to solve problems and the more we feel alive. Eventually we will discover that the energy and vitality we feel is because we are becoming increasingly aware of a power greater than ourselves. We will discover that a consciousness of God is more than the answer to our problems; it is life itself. To be alive is to be aware of the Creator. It is to know the truth of our own being.

This may be a concept that is difficult for us to grasp. This is acceptable. In fact, it is advisable, because being totally alive transcends mental concepts. A consciousness of God is not only an avenue through which answers to challenges can emerge, but also a kind of glass through which we see the world. It also gives rise to different behaviors. We find ourselves doing things we have not done before. We are more understanding, less tense, more creative and loving. In short, a consciousness of God transforms us into a door through which a divine potential is expressed.

DAY 29

Jesus said, "I am the gate" (Jn. 10:9). During a time of contemplation today, meditate upon this statement. Reread what was written for Day 29 and record your thoughts below.

DAY 29

I am the wick of the candle.

I have an experiment for you. Take a small candle and remove the wick, and then try to light it. You will find this extremely difficult if not impossible. The stored light and heat are present in the wax of the candle, but they are not accessible without the wick.

God has the same challenge. Love, peace, strength and wisdom are available to the human family, but like a candle, a "wick" is required. From this day forth, let us remember that we were created to be a wick in the candle that is God's presence and power. However, before we can experience the light and love of the Presence, we must be immersed in God. In other words, we must become aware of the Spirit that dwells in us.

This is the genius of God at work. Once we awaken to the Presence, a wick is provided so that the fullness and allness of God can flow into our experience. Dear friend, remember the simplicity of God's plan. We were created as points of awareness in the same way that a candle is a point of light. One of us conscious of Spirit becomes an avenue for God's expression.

DAY 30

Imagine being high above the earth and gazing at the dark shrouded continents of the night. There are no lights. Suddenly there is a single light. Someone has just become a wick in God's candle. Another light captures your attention, and then another. Where there was only one, now there are thousands.

Could it be that someone looking at Earth from this vantage point would eventually witness a planet without a night, for God's light shines so brightly? Write your thoughts as you consider the possibilities of all of us realizing our full potential as wicks in the candle of the Lord.

DAY 30

God is calling me.

Humanity has been calling God for eons. We want Spirit to descend to the earth and do the work that we have not been able to do. We call on God to provide a job for us or at least enough money to meet our current financial crisis. We want God to heal our bodies. Always our prayer is for God's intervention on earth and in our earthly affairs. Perhaps there is a better way, God's way.

While we have been calling for God to descend, God has been calling for us to ascend, to rise in consciousness so that we can experience the presence and power of God, with no lack and nothing to heal. If we can touch the hem of this garment, all will be well.

I think we know that God is not answering our call to descend into our human world. The question is "Will we answer God's call to rise up in consciousness and become aware of the Presence that has made a home in us?"

I speculate that you have already answered God's call, for you have been praying and meditating and waiting for Grace to take you to the summit of the mountain or for the Holy Spirit wind to lift your outstretched wings and carry you to a height where you can see clearly. (See Step 7 for a review of "The High Meadow" and "Putting on Your Wings.")

In the space provided, indicate the prayer practice you have been using as you answer God's call.

DAY 31

I am waiting ...

Waiting is the heart of The Gathering, but there are those who would say that it accomplishes little or nothing. They demand action, which they believe is necessary. Their belief is half true. Action is called for in life, but not always by us. Waiting invites the activity of Spirit, and therefore it is not us, but God who changes the world.

Waiting is our way of saying "stop" to ourselves. We cease trying to bring our vision into the world so that a divine vision can fill our minds and engage our willingness to become instruments of a divine will.

When we first wait, we become like children again, unable to sit still. The world calls to us, and we want to run to and fro. Our minds know nothing of the present moment and think about the past and future.

Wait for a time and you will discover that there is much activity in you that you have hidden from yourself. Wait for a few minutes and you will quickly discover the thoughts that constantly move within you. This awareness, although sometimes unsettling, is a treasure, for it is self-awareness. It is an answer to the philosopher's call to "Know thyself."

Pause for a few minutes and become a watcher. Simply observe the thoughts and feelings that are alive in you. Take note of them and briefly record them in the space below. Dear friend, you are beginning to know yourself.

DAY 32

I am waiting ... still.

Yesterday the waiting began with the simple act of observation. It did not matter what we discovered was moving within us. It was most important that we acknowledged that there is movement in us. Thoughts are present. Feelings are living in us. Images are fellow companions. There are dreams and regrets. Inside us is the dwelling place of many residents.

When we wait, there is the tendency to call some of what lives in us good and desirable, while other parts of us are condemned. Consider for a moment if someone condemned us—what would we do? What would be our tendency? Most likely we would shy away from the condemner. This is happening within us as hidden parts of ourselves erupt at inopportune times and ambush us. This is why we wait and judge not.

The thoughts, feelings and images that live in us are not to be condemned. They are to be accepted as they are. Condemnation fosters resistance, and resistance serves as a veil through which we see dimly. Not only do parts of us remain unknown to us, but we do not see the world clearly.

Today the real work begins: watching without condemnation. In the space below, indicate your current ability to encounter parts of your interior world without condemnation. Don't condemn yourself, but honestly state if you were able to observe without judgment. If this was difficult, don't be concerned, for tomorrow's activity will help you enter a consciousness beyond good and bad.

DAY 33

Still waiting …

Waiting requires detachment. This is difficult when we seem to sit in a vortex of thoughts, feelings and memories. We try to swat them away as if they were a squadron of mosquitoes persistently seeking something from us we are not willing to give. The vortex can convince us that we are not "cut out" for waiting and stillness. We affirm once more we are people of action.

We may be people of action, but many of the things we do originate in human consciousness rather than an awareness of Spirit. Dear friend, there is a way to detach from the thoughts, feelings, images and memories that plague us. The answer lies in six words: *It is; God is; I am.*

It is helps us resist the human tendency to label thoughts, feelings, images and memories as good or bad. As the vortex begins to subside, we turn to God with the simple two-word mantra *God is*. This is probably the purest statement we can make about the Creator. This God is beyond description and by affirming *God is* we draw closer to the pure being of Spirit. This is where we wait—a state of mind and heart beyond labels. Here even God is free from our judgment.

Finally we come to ourselves, not the one who tends to label, but the pure creation of God, the one

- - - - - - -

who bears God's name—*I am*. Speak the six words and then wait. Detach from the exterior world, and then detach from the interior world of thought, feelings, images and memories. When we are free of these worlds, we just may find ourselves living in the kingdom of God, aware of the indwelling presence and power God is.

During your time of prayer and meditation, be willing to enter the vortex if it appears, and if you do, let the six-word mantra help you detach from what a part of you would want to resist. In the space below, record any insights about the practice. In fact, you might want to share these insights with other friends who are a part of your gathering group.

DAY 34

I am discovering what God wants me to have.

I must admit I have not given much thought to what God wants me to have. In the past, I set my goals and hoped they were in alignment with some mysterious, unfolding divine plan for my life. Now I am beginning to realize that one of life's great goals is contentment. Of course, one approach to contentment is dependent upon events. If I get what I want, I am content ... for a while.

Paul, writing to the Philippians, opens a door to another way of life: "For I have learned, in whatever state I am, to be content" (Phil. 4:11 RSV). Imagine facing stressful situations from a consciousness of contentment. It does not matter whether we act with boldness and daring or whether we take a passive approach to our challenge, contentment rules the day. Our soul longs for this way of life.

The Gathering prayer and meditation practice is designed to prepare us to receive this gift. Today is the day to set aside other hoped-for desires and to open ourselves to one of the greatest gifts a person can receive—contentment without condition.

This experience can be shocking for us. We find ourselves in a situation that is usually charged with emotion—for instance, a meeting with our ex-spouse—but we are peaceful. The meeting doesn't go

DAY 35

our way, but we are content. The mantra of past days is becoming our life—*It is; God is; I am.* I wonder if Paul used such a six-word phrase on his way to discovering what God wanted him to have.

Has there been a time in your life when a condition consistently troubled you? Did you find the detached contentment that Paul wrote about in his letter to the Philippians? Is there a similar situation in your life today? How will you find contentment?

DAY 35

I have learned, in whatever state I am, to be content.

A Gathering has at its heart what is in our heart, the quest to be conscious of the presence of God. There can be a long, arduous journey before we acknowledge that this is what we want. The world is alluring and calls out to us like the sirens of ancient Greek myth. If we respond to this voice, we eventually find ourselves in shallow water and on the rocks. This, of course, is a sign that we have been off course for some time.

Just as there is a sign that tells us our life is not working, there is also a sign that tells us our course is true and fair weather lies ahead. The sign is contentment, a contentment and sense of fulfillment that does not depend upon circumstance. This is what is so stunning about this sign. The seas may be turbulent, but our souls are at rest.

Remember the story of Jesus asleep in a boat on the Sea of Galilee? The disciples became concerned for their safety when a storm came upon them. Jesus was awakened to calm the stormy sea, but it is evident to the reader of this story that there was no fear in him. The circumstance may have been dire, but Jesus was content, and his peaceful consciousness calmed the waters.

DAY 36

- - - - - - -

Is there a circumstance in your life that continues to trouble you? You face this circumstance or person periodically. Describe the circumstance below.

This situation that has generated turmoil is now going to be used to help you determine if The Gathering practice is working in your life. The regularity of the circumstance is an opportunity for self-observation to determine if you are becoming more peaceful and content. The hope is that you will eventually be content even if you find yourself in the midst of the condition.

As you observe yourself, you will discover that the intensity of the emotions lessens and that there are times when the contentment is present, although its life can be short-lived. Remember the day is coming when the contentment you feel will remain. When this happens, return to this page and write the date below. You might want to bookmark the page as a reminder that you are to return once you find yourself in the calm waters of contentment.

DAY 36

■ ■ ■ ■ ■ ■ ■

God is enough.

God is enough is one of my favorite affirmations. There is nothing wrong with having friends to support you, but one of the joys of life is discovering the inner God-given resources necessary for radiant living. At times, we lean too heavily upon other people as our deliverer. This is a time to declare *God is enough.*

I can assure you that there is great comfort in these three words. There is a purity that I love. They remind me to look within myself for the resources necessary to live my life. There are few things more important than finding these "natural" resources.

I wonder, at times, if the eternal quest myths that form part of many cultures are not a call to discover ourselves and the treasure that is within us. A hero may travel to distant places and face many challenges. A treasure can be won, but it is the adventure itself that is of greatest value because it has uncovered him; it has helped him discover his inner resources.

The mythical heroes were on a holy quest and so are we. In fact, all of life is such a journey, but for most of us it looks ordinary. We call it forgiveness or finding a job or getting up again after we have fallen. Properly viewed, these life circumstances reach into our minds and hearts and demand that we stand on our own feet and live our lives as if *God is enough*.

As you practice the principles of The Gathering in your personal meditative life, give attention to the three words *God is enough*. For the next seven days, let the "time beyond time" portion of your Gathering be centered on the phrase *God is enough*. Wait and rest with these words, and let them reveal to you their depth and implications. Please record your insights and discoveries below.

DAY 37

I remember it is a consciousness of God I seek.

The spiritual life is vast and varied. It challenges us to accept ourselves as we are and to let go of the world, but we must be cautious that the joys and consolations of the spiritual life do not replace the pleasures and wants of an earthly life. Human beings tend to move from one form of attachment to another rather than to live in freedom.

Prayer and meditation, even the experience of a Gathering, can be addictive. We feel better, our life is changing, people see us differently, we are more confident, we are discovering hidden talents, and forgiving ourselves and others. We see the parallel between the steps of The Gathering and the changes that are taking place in our lives.

During this period of inner transformation, it is important to remember we seek a consciousness of God. It was Jesus who said that if we seek the kingdom, everything else will be added to us. Even joy, peace, insights and feelings are "added things." It is a consciousness of God we want. We seek it, and then allow it to manifest itself in whatever manner it will. In this way, we maintain a purity of intent. This is why the first reminder is to be shared at each Gathering, for we are not to focus on the blessings of

* * * * * * *

an awareness of God's presence; we are to give thanks that we can know the One.

What blessings are beginning to be made manifest in your life? Have you found yourself focusing upon the added things? If you have experienced this, forgive yourself and return to your purpose of wakefulness. Being awake to God is enough.

DAY 38

All is well.

We seek goals and pursue dreams. Sometimes they are realized; sometimes they are not. When we strive and fail, we usually think less of ourselves. Our confidence plummets, and if we set more goals they are sometimes less lofty than before. It is more difficult for us to believe that life's promises have been promised to us. This is true when we engage in earthly pursuits, but it is also true when we earnestly begin a spiritual life.

As you put the principles and ideals of The Gathering to the test, you will find waiting to be the most challenging "goal" of your life. Day after day, you will wonder why you are doing this. You will hear an inner voice, the voice of your human self, telling you that these steps don't work and that you are wasting your time. Nearly everyone who ventures into the depths of the human self experiences these thoughts and the feelings that go with them. Expect them. You will not be the first person to circumnavigate them. Instead you are another person in a long line of dedicated individuals who is giving yourself to a way of life. This is the key. You are not setting goals; you are committing to a way of life.

When you find yourself grading your quiet time, pause and listen for the voice of God in you saying, "What you seek is a way of life. Every step, every seeming failure from which you rise to try again builds a foundation for your life of prayer and meditation.

Bring to mind the image of a child learning to walk. The little one first pulls himself up supported by a mother's hand or by a table. Steps are taken, and his balance is lost. Do you think the child places cosmic significance on his failure to walk? Does the child begin to believe he will never walk and cease to try to stand erect? Perhaps, in a language the child understands, the Creator whispers in his ear, "All is well; take another step."

Become like a child, and when you hear the voice of your lower self telling you what you cannot do, listen for another voice, the voice of the One who spoke to you when you were learning to walk. Long ago it said, "All is well; take another step." Surely you will once again hear the Creator say, "All is well," followed by encouraging words. Write the encouraging words below.

DAY 39

* * * * * * *

I gather in God's name.

It is said that loneliness is our greatest pain. It is what we fear most. Isn't it strange that in order to know we are not alone we must be alone? Even when the principles of The Gathering are practiced by a group of people, there is still a time of aloneness when we are in company with only our thoughts, feelings, memories and images of our minds.

In this moment of being alone, the person who gathers is linked not only with the members of his or her group, but also with those who are not a part of a gathering group. In truth, it is impossible to gather alone because there are people around the world who are united in this prayer and meditation practice called The Gathering.

What unites us is that we gather in God's name; we are joined in a unique understanding of God's nature and the nature of the spiritual life. This does not happen by accident. Consciousness silently calls out to others of like mind with the same yearning hearts and asks them to join in oneness with Spirit. Once this is experienced, it is natural to say, *We have gathered in God's name. This is what is important. We will gather again.*

Sit quietly during your next Gathering and open yourself to the shared experience of the gatherers around the world. Can you sense that you are not alone? Is there any way you can put your feeling into words? Begin to write and see what flows from your pen.

DAY 40

The Gathering

How to Form and
Conduct a Gathering

To have friends is to experience wealth beyond measure and to have access to wisdom that is greater than the sum of the minds that gather. When spiritual friends come together, a principle revealed by Jesus is enacted: "For where two or three are gathered in my name, I am there among them" (Mt. 18:20).

When friends come together with the intent of expressing their divine nature and committing themselves to a spiritual way of life, something greater than the sum of the individuals emerges from their hearts and minds—an indwelling Presence. Always at rest within us, it waits for us to forget ourselves. We can then give attention to a power greater than ourselves and to people who may seem separate from us, but who we instinctively know are a part of us.

A Gathering is a group of spiritual friends blessing one another and through their collective consciousness blessing the world. If you observed a Gathering from afar, you would see people from all walks of life arriving at an individual's home, a house of worship, a park where blankets are placed

■ ■ ■ ■ ■ ■ ■

on the ground, or a circle of chairs under the stars. Where a circle can be formed, a Gathering can come into being.

Obviously two or three people can form a Gathering, but so can seven friends; maybe even the mystical number of 12 individuals can join to form a Gathering. If more than 12 people want to gather, it is best to create a second Gathering to insure a reasonable amount of time to complete the nine steps of the prayer practice.

After reading *The Gathering* and sensing the possibilities of personal and global transformation, a single person may yearn to form a Gathering. One of the first questions will be who to ask to join the group. Inviting a like-minded friend who is spiritually oriented is a good beginning. The two friends can meet, look over this book, and consider if this is a journey they want to take. Other names can be introduced and the process of The Gathering explained to other potential gatherers.

Since a consciousness of the presence of God is the purpose for a Gathering, it is most important that those who share the experience have a propensity for prayer and meditation. Open-mindedness is also a prerequisite because, as you are aware, some of the foundation principles of The Gathering will challenge the mind. I look for three qualities in a potential gatherer: attention to prayer and meditation as a way of life, belief in spiritual exploration, and spiritual strength to follow through on commitments.

Once the individuals express their intention to gather, a regular meeting time is selected, perhaps once a week or every other week. Meeting only once a month is probably not enough time to build the consciousness necessary to fully experience the promise of a Gathering.

One person should be responsible for a single Gathering. The responsibility can be passed from one gatherer to another depending on how often the group gathers. This individual will greet those who come and help to establish a sacred and reverent consciousness by lighting candles, playing meditative music, and greeting those who come. There may be refreshments or even a class of some kind after a Gathering, but it is good to share The Gathering prayer and meditation practice first.

Once everyone is welcomed and the circle is formed, the day's leader will initiate The Gathering. When I start a gathering, I usually lead the group in deep breathing or a short relaxation meditation before asking the person on my left to begin with Step 1. Then we proceed clockwise from person to person until Step 1 returns to me as I declare, *I release my human need.*

The Gathering continues according to the process outlined in the book under the various sections

■ ■ ■ ■ ■ ■ ■

entitled "Taking the Step." Remember, Steps 1 through 5 are spoken individually by each gatherer. Step 6 is affirmed in unison by all the people present. Step 7 is the heart of The Gathering, where the facilitator will lead the group into the "time beyond time," dominated by waiting, trusting and listening.

When I lead a Gathering, I usually select through prayer and meditation a theme for the "time beyond time." For instance, the focus might be upon the idea *God is enough,* or *As the sun rises in the east, the Spirit of God is rising in my soul.* The meditation of perhaps 10 to 20 minutes would give attention to ideas such as these, followed by periods of waiting, punctuated with brief statements such as the ones above. There may even be a time, Christmas, for instance, when the focusing element would be a lighted candle placed in the center of the circle.

As the "time beyond time" is nearing its conclusion, the leader will gently lead The Gathering to an awareness of the world once more. I usually ask everyone to take a deep breath, listen for a sound and open his or her eyes just enough to see light and then close the eyes once more. I then gently affirm Step 8: *I have learned, in whatever state I am, to be content. God is enough,* and ask the gatherers to join me in declaring Step 8. I say, "Let's share Step 8 together." The word "together" is to be a call for all to join with me

- - - - - - - -

in the step. The Gathering concludes as the leader reads the Three Reminders.

Dear friend, I urge you to form a Gathering and experience its joys. It can be a relatively short beginning or conclusion to a day, or it can be the start of an extended time of spiritual sharing. The Gathering can stand alone or support other activities selected by the group.

The key factor is a unity of Spirit of those who gather. Imagine the growth to be experienced and the power unleashed by spiritual seekers united by an allegiance to the practice of prayer and meditation, joined by a need to explore the mysteries of the Infinite, and whose commitment to such endeavors is unwavering.

* * * * * * * *

The Gathering

Conclusion

Long ago a psalmist captured the spirit of The Gathering: "How good and how pleasant it is for brethren to dwell together in unity" (Ps. 133:1 NKJV). Through reading, you are nearing the end of *The Gathering*, but you are just beginning to put to the test the principles outlined in the steps of The Gathering prayer and meditation practice. Now is the time to take note of the current state of your life.

Are you healthy? Are you energetic? Does energy flow from within you that is sufficient for each task, or do you find it difficult to begin an endeavor because you are tired and listless?

Are your relationships healthy? Do you share life with good friends? Are there people with whom you regularly communicate your deepest thoughts, feelings and dreams?

Are there unresolved relationships from the past? Does anger flare up from within you with only slight provocation? Have you built a fence to protect yourself from hurt only to find it hems you in?

Are you living a life of purpose and moving ahead with faith into the unknown, or are you fearful of tomorrow and simply hanging on to what you

■ ■ ■ ■ ■ ■ ■

currently have? Do you feel limited, or do you sense a wonderful potential in you to be expressed?

Do you easily entertain new ideas, or are you set in your ways? Is there something you have always wanted to do, but now you can hardly remember what it is?

These questions are presented to you with the hope that they help you determine the current state of your life. It does not matter how you answer the questions or whether your answers indicate a person eager to embrace change or one afraid to step out of limitation. The key is to note the current state of your life. Nothing else is required; however, in one year, I want you to assess your life again.

Through The Gathering prayer and meditation process, we are not only exploring an approach to daily living; we are also putting principles and ideals to the test. After one year, the effect of The Gathering practice will be evident. It will either support the expression of your potential, or it will not. Some might say, "time will tell," but time is not the issue. The question is whether over the course of the next 365 days, you give The Gathering a fair chance to do its sacred work.

Dear friend, nothing of consequence happens in our lives without commitment. I have concluded that *commitment* is the most important word in our language. Halfhearted application gets mixed results.

· · · · · · · ·

Full commitment is a gift we give ourselves because it assures us that the best that is possible is made manifest. When I think about my life, I see a recurring theme. I don't do anything halfway. Full immersion is my way of life.

From time to time I have taught what I call a breakthrough or commitment class. Such a course usually lasts six weeks. It is limited to 25 people. Before joining, a person must commit to being present at all classes. If an individual is going to be on vacation and miss one of the sessions, it is not his time. The breakthrough class also requires that a person stand and speak during each class and do homework as well. (I like to call the homework "own work," for it is truly ours to do.) If a person does not think she or he can do this, it is not their time.

What I have discovered is that these classes are transformative in a way that most classes are not. I have wondered what the difference is between a breakthrough class and a typical class. Obviously there is the work and expression of each student during each of the six weeks of the experience, but I am convinced that the most powerful contributor to transformation is commitment. There is a vast difference between *I think I'll check out this class* and *I am dedicating myself to a spiritual breakthrough for the next six weeks of my life.*

. . . .

I can assure you that if you make a commitment to The Gathering prayer and meditation practice, in one year when you do an assessment of your life, you will be amazed. In fact, you might want to answer the probing questions above, put them in an envelope, seal it and place it at the back of your book. Write on the envelope the date it was sealed. Also, write that in one year the envelope is to be opened, but only after the probing questions are answered once more.

In one year, open the envelope and compare / contrast the status of your life a year ago to where it has progressed because of your commitment to The Gathering. Dear friend, if I could be everywhere present, I would love to be present when the envelope is opened for each of you who has done this work. What a joy it would be to witness your amazement and delight in what has happened first in your interior life and then what has happened in your world. Perhaps it is true to say that the greatest delight will not be because certain things have happened as much as the way you are now observing and experiencing what is happening.

If I were to make a prediction, I'd prophesize you are less concerned about what happens to you than you are about what happens in you, that you are less concerned with happenings because it is evident that you are a happening in the world. What I mean is that life is not what happens to you; your life is not an effect, but rather a cause of a greater good in the world.

Within one year, I believe you will discover this new vision whether you are part of a Gathering group or you test the principles in your own contemplative life. On that day of the new vision, when you know you are a happening in the world, think back to the beginning when you first dared to say, *I release my human need*.

· · ■ · ■ · ■ · ■ · ■ · ■ · ■

The Gathering

Endnotes

Step 1

1. Joel S. Goldsmith, *A Parenthesis in Eternity* (New York: Harper and Row, ©1963, 1986).

2. H. Emilie Cady, *How I Used Truth* (Kansas City, MO: Unity School of Christianity, 1941).

Step 7

1. Matthew Fox, *Meditations With Meister Eckhart* (Santa Fe, NM: Bear and Company, 1983).

The Gathering

About the Author

Prior to entering the ministry, Jim Rosemergy served as an aviator in the United States Navy and as a navigator on an RA-5C Vigilante reconnaissance jet stationed aboard the USS Kitty Hawk. He flew more than 100 combat missions over North Vietnam.

Ordained a Unity minister in 1976, Rev. Rosemergy has served ministries in Raleigh, North Carolina; Spokane, Washington; Kansas City, Missouri; Sunrise Beach, Missouri; and is currently the senior minister of Unity of Fort Myers, Florida. Jim's focus in ministry is spiritual awakening and his writings reflect this approach to life.

A previous columnist for *Unity Magazine*, he is also the author of 15 books, including *Even Mystics Have Bills to Pay*, *The Quest for Meaning* and *Attaining the Unattainable: The Will of God*. In addition, he is a contributing author to *New Thought for a New Millennium*.

Jim has served the Association of Unity Churches International (now Unity Worldwide Ministries) during his ministerial career, been elected to the Board of Directors and Executive Committee, and during 1987–88, he served as president of the Association. He is the recipient of the Association's 2007 Light of God Expressing Award. In addition, he served the

Unity movement as an executive vice president of Unity School of Christianity from 1990 to 2001. Jim is a popular speaker at Unity churches and centers, as well as at other New Thought spiritual events.

Jim and his wife, Nancy, have two grown, married sons and two granddaughters. Athletic all his life, Jim enjoys golfing and kayaking.

For more information about Jim Rosemergy,

please visit jimrosemergy.com